Kara-Leah Grant's commitment to you and Yoga is astounding. She is holding your hand and leading you to the healing power of intimate connection. Kara-Leah is persisting and insisting that you can be completely intimate with the pure intelligence and beauty of your life. Your Yoga practice will be actual, natural, non obsessive and daily! It is your direct embrace of the wonder that is your own reality. Let Kara-Leah lead you in this adventure that will transform you and transfigure you to the light and love that is our natural state.

~ **Mark Whitwell, author of *Yoga of Heart* and *The Promise***

A wonderful primer for the hesitant beginning yogi, offering a wealth of information in Kara-Leah's inimitable, accessible style.

~ **Kelly Fisher, Director of Urban Yoga, Wellington**

I often say to my students that the hardest part of yoga is actually getting on your mat. In this book Kara-Leah helps you to break through some of that resistance that may be holding you back, plus it's a great go-to book to understand more about the practice of yoga, history, myths and styles. In Kara-Leah's trademark no-nonsense approach, she manages to keep things clear and interesting, communicating from her first hand experience - she has literally been there as the student and experienced the full spectrum of the yo [ ] *book is a perfect companion for the modern yogi. As* [ ] *'This shift of consciousness is available to every on* [ ] *natural evolution of a human being.'*

~ **Nikki Ralston, *The*** [ ]

This book is easy to read as a glass of water is [ ] *a hot day. And just as valuable. Kara-Leah's word* [ ] *p wisdom that is the result of a life lived authentic* [ ] *at wisdom, the essence of Yoga, generously, and I am pr* [ ] *ve been one of the first to read it.*

~ **Ben Ralston, Healer, Yoga Teacher, Writer**

This will be a great tool for people who just can't seem to get started with yoga. Written from experience Kara-Leah gives you numerous ways to get past the road blocks that seem to prevent many people from walking into their first yoga class. It gives insights into many misconceptions about yoga, and answers numerous questions about terminology that may baffle. The 200 pages are set out in a methodical and insightful manner, and will keep you on track to enjoy the many benefits that regular yoga will bring to your life.

~ Colin Clements, Australia Yoga Life

A Yoga teacher needs to be humble enough to continue their own journey of learning and healing, and brave enough to share it with those they teach. Kara-Leah shares her learning in a lighthearted, clear and accessible way. There is reassurance and advice for the novice yogi, further detail for the experienced Yogi and reminders for teachers too.

~ Gemma Carroll, Akasha Yoga Studio, Dunedin NZ

I have been steeped in spiritual practice since early childhood and have witnessed the exponential growth of yoga as an industry in the US, and also abroad, as I've been living and teaching overseas since 1999. We in the Western world are now blessed with a wide variety of choice. This enables each individual to align with the most suitable practice, at any given time, for him or her. However, this blessing of choice also becomes the challenge to know where to go, before you go. How do you know what to look for when this world of yoga is new to you? And as yoga becomes more of a marketplace, how can you separate the gold from the dross? I've had the pleasure of coming to know Kara-Leah over the past six years and I've seen close-up how she lives the process that is Yoga. In her latest book, she supports you in stepping safely and confidently into the ever-changing stream of Yoga. This is a valuable go-to manual for anyone confounded by not only the glittering new yoga, but also the complexities of the ancient yoga. Dive in, and welcome to the journey!

~ Melissa Billington, creatrix of MYOGA—freedom to unfold, melissabillington.com

The NO-MORE-EXCUSES Guide to YOGA

Enjoy!
Many blessings!

Also by Kara-Leah Grant

Forty Days of Yoga

The NO-MORE-EXCUSES Guide to YOGA

Because Yoga is for every body

KARA-LEAH GRANT

Aarohati
Publishing

Aarohati
Publishing

256 Queens Drive
Lyall Bay
Wellington 6022

National Library of New Zealand Cataloguing-in-Publication Data

Grant, Kara-Leah, 1975-
The no-more-excuses guide to yoga : because yoga is for every
body / Kara-Leah Grant.
ISBN 978-0-473-29537-0—978-0-473-29539-4
1. Yoga. I. Title.
181.45—dc 23

Cover: Kelly Spencer
Print production: Matthew Bartlett

Dedication

This book is dedicated to the wisest part of all of us, that part which has lead you here today. The yogis call it the Atman; you might call it your intuition, your soul, or your heart. All names aside, it is the spark of divinity that we all share, that which connects us heart to heart around the globe.

CONTENTS

6. IN CLASS 161

CONCLUSION: FINDING TIME, MAKING TIME, HANGING IN THERE

ACKNOWLEDGEMENTS

ABOUT THE AUTHOR

INTRODUCTION: WHAT IS YOGA?

W elcome to the world of Yoga – a place where we use our bodies to explore our psyches and gain mastery over our minds.

Whether you've already done a few classes and want to know more about yoga, or you've never taken a class in your life, you're in the right place.

Heck, maybe you're not ready at all and have been talking about trying yoga for years, but something always got in the way. Instead of trying yoga, you thought you might read a book about it instead. Even if that's you... you're still in the right place. It's my aim to blast through all those excuses you have about why you haven't started practicing and get you into class and onto a yoga mat.

After reading this book, you'll have no more excuses to keep you out of the yoga room.

On a much sneakier level, this book also attempts to give you a taste of yoga so in the *act* of reading it you are actually practicing yoga. Sometimes I'll ask you to stop and breathe in a certain way, sometimes I'll ask you what's going on in your head right now and if you can watch those thoughts without identifying with them. Sometimes I might even ask you to meditate for a moment or two. This is all yoga, because as it's about to become abundantly clear, yoga is far more than just the practice of physical postures.

You may still be unsure about trying this yoga thing – maybe you think you're too inflexible or too old or too big or too male. These are common misconceptions people can have about yoga and I plan to demolish them one by one. Along the way I'll also answer some of the most common questions I hear from people who want to start yoga.

After that, we'll take a look at the history and the philosophy of yoga as well as the concepts you may come across in class. I'll tell you all about the practice of yoga and what that might include because yoga is not just about bending and stretching into funny looking postures.

We'll investigate teachers, classes and studios so you know how to find a great teacher and what warning signs to look out for – not all teachers are good teachers and some are downright bad. I'll lead you by the hand into your first yoga class so you can feel comfortable, keep yourself safe, and understand the many strange things that are a part of yoga.

There is a lot of material to cover, but you don't have to read it all in one go. There may be some chapters that don't apply to you. For this reason, this book is more like a reference book – each chapter is designed to stand alone.

Most of you will have come to this book with an idea that yoga equals yoga postures. This is like living next to a harbour your entire life and thinking that the water contained inside the harbour is the ocean. One day, you board a ship and sail out of the harbour and discover to your amazement that *this* is the ocean. For most of us asana – or postures – are our first port of call when it comes to yoga. That's where we start and it's a fantastic place to start. Why? Because most of us are so disconnected from our bodies that we desperately need to practice asana so we can learn to live inside our bodies again.

But this is not where yoga ends, and while this book devotes plenty of its pages talking about asana, asana classes, asana teachers it is written from the perspective of Yoga as the ocean – not the harbour.

When I'm talking about Yoga with a capital Y, I'm talking about Yoga as a process where one learns to be fully present with the moment.

'Yoga is the journey of the Self, through the Self, to the Self.'*

That's all. And the *practice* of yoga (small y) is what we *do*, ourselves, as we journey through ourselves, to ourselves. That practice is asana – but it's also pranayama, meditation, chanting and practices included on paths like Karma Yoga.

Practicing asana teaches us about yoga until finally we live our lives from a total state of Yoga – a state of presence.

But don't worry too much about whether you get this or not at this point. You don't have to get it... it's just an introduction so that you can start asking questions. Because that is a big part of yoga – inquiring into your experience.

Many of us are looking for answers to life's big questions – Who am I? What do I want? What's my purpose? What's the point of life? Where am I going?

Yoga is one way to explore these questions... that's the beginning of the journey of the Self. It's a journey that ultimately starts with our bodies – not our minds. Because while our minds can spin all sorts of thoughts and beliefs about the way we are and the way the world is, our body is grounded in the here and now. Our body is as it is. It will tell us the truth, from moment to moment.

In essence our body doesn't just *house* our mind or psyche – it *is* our mind or psyche. The practice of yoga as we mostly know it in the West – physical postures – affects our body, which in turn affects our psyche. In simple terms, this is why breathing mindfully

---

* It's likely this is a translation of 13:24 of *The Bhagavad Gita* – the text it is attributed to.

> *By meditation, some men*
> *can see the Self in the self;*
> *others, by the yoga of knowledge;*
> *others, by selfless action.* (translation Stephen Mitchell)

while moving our body can have such a profound effect. It's why Yoga can lead to an awakening of Self and a shift in consciousness as we realise we are not the small separate limited ego-self we've always believed, but actually an infinite, connected part of a larger whole.

This shift of consciousness is not reserved for the most dedicated of yoga practitioners or those with the most perfect of postures, or the most committed pranayama or lengthiest meditations. This shift of consciousness is available to every one of us – it is the natural evolution of a human being. We will all wake up to our inherent inter-connectedness, one day or another.

Self-realisation is ultimately what yoga is all about – realising the Self. For today though, your yoga could be all about lengthening your hamstrings, opening your shoulders, building strength, or losing weight.

That is enough. The rest, it doesn't matter. It's always there, waiting for you when you're ready. But just knowing before you go to your first class that yoga is about more than forward bends, twists and backbends gives you some context for what might happen in class, or inside of you.

So step forth into the world of yoga, knowing that it will meet you where you are, and you can take as much or as little as you like from the practice. Know that nothing is asked of you except that you show up, that you are curious, and that you stay open to your experience. Forget everything you think you may know and be like a child again – curious, open and enthusiastic about exploring. That is where Yoga will meet you, and that is where this book will take you.

First though, we're going to blast through some of those misconceptions that might be keeping you off the yoga mat and out of the yoga class.

1. COMMON MISCONCEPTIONS ABOUT YOGA

I'm not flexible enough to do yoga

Of all the reasons why people don't practice yoga, this is the most strange. It's laugh-out loud weird.

Why don't you practice yoga? Oh – I'm not flexible enough. Not flexible enough? That's like saying... why don't you go grocery shopping? Because my cupboards are too empty. Or why don't you have a shower? Because I'm too dirty.

Flexibility is not a pre-requisite for yoga, it's a *by-product* of yoga practice.

I'm going to say that again because it's key to this entire yoga experience.

Flexibility is not a pre-requisite for yoga, it's a *by-product* of yoga practice.

There's a huge difference there. Although I totally relate to the 'I'm Not Flexible Enough for Yoga Camp'. Once upon a time, that was me. I was completely and totally inflexible. In fact, I'd be willing to bet I was far less flexible then, than you are right now – if this were a competition, which it's not. How do I know? Because in all my years of teaching yoga, I have never seen one person come into class who was as inflexible as I was when I started yoga – and I've taught all kinds of beginners.

In high school Physical Education (P.E.) we were given stan-dardised testing every year to see how fit we were. Two decades later, I can't remember how we were tested for strength or fitness, but I sure can remember how we were tested for flexibility.

We had to sit down on our bottoms, legs out straight in front of us, and a special ruler was placed at our feet with the numbers one through seven marked out. If you could only reach your fingertips to the one, you had the worst flexibility ever; reach the seven and you had the best flexibility. I remember doing this test when I was 13 and again at 14 (after that, P.E. wasn't compulsory). Both times, I couldn't even get on the scale. I was off-the-scale inflexible.

So I get it. I get how it feels to be inflexibility and that is how I know that the best thing you can do for your inflexibility is to take yourself to a yoga class – the right class with the right teacher, as melting that tension will take time. But it will happen. With patience, and persistence, in time you will become more flexible. I'm living proof of that.

Now, when I hear people say 'I'm not flexible enough to do yoga', what I hear is:

'I'm afraid of looking stiff and uncomfortable in class.'

'I'm afraid of being stiff and uncomfortable – as long as I stick to my usual range of movement I don't have to be reminded of how stiff and uncomfortable I really am.'

I hear people saying:

'I don't want to look like an idiot or a fool, the stiff one amongst all these bendy folk.'

'I don't want to stick out or look like I can't do it.'

'I don't want people to laugh at me, or pity me, or wonder what on earth I'm doing in a yoga class.'

That's what I hear you saying, and those are all valid thoughts and feelings. Now we're getting to the crux of the matter.

Why don't you do yoga? It's not that you're not flexible enough, it's that you're *afraid* of how doing yoga might make you feel – in the short-term.

It can be difficult to imagine how yoga might make you feel in the long-term. How about bendy? Soft? Surrendered? At ease? Relaxed? Open? How about that? Is that how you would like to feel when you reach over to tie up your shoelaces or get down on the floor to play with your kids or grandkids?

Ironically, while yoga is about self-acceptance and meeting you where you are – whether you are tight and inflexible or open and bendy – yoga class is still a place where we can feel easily ashamed of our bodies. It can become just one more place where we beat ourselves up because we don't fit the ideal we have got in our heads.

Who wants to go and do something that makes them feel ashamed of their body?

Nobody.

So the inflexible avoid yoga class and stay inflexible. In many ways, the yoga actually starts *before* you go to class. It starts with inquiring into yourself around this idea of flexibility and inflexibility. Now that you know you don't have to be flexible to go to class, are you chomping at the bit to get yourself to the very next available yoga class... or are you still reluctant and holding back? If you're still reluctant, what are you afraid of?

Ask yourself these questions and see what answers float up. Dig down deep and get to the bottom of this reluctance. Understand that behind that reluctance lies fear, and that fear is always a huge flashing neon sign that says: "Something to See Here." Fear is a pointer that shows us where we need to go in life – what we need to turn toward and face.

Now I'm not talking about the kind of fear you feel when you're down a dark alley and a menacing guy drops into step behind you. The kind of fear that comes up then is telling you to run like hell to save your bacon.

Problem is, we usually confuse the different kinds of fear we experience. Fear of an immediate situation is necessary for survival. Whereas psychological fear reveals what we need to do become a more healthy person.

Psychological fear starts with acknowledging how you feel. It starts with acknowledging all of your feelings. It's okay to feel afraid; to feel worried about being embarrassed or worried about what other people will think. It's okay to be worried about not being able to keep up with the class, or to be concerned about hurting yourself, or anxious about pushing yourself too far.

These are legitimate feelings that serve a purpose – the purpose of those feelings and worries is to tell you what you *need* to get out of a yoga class.

First, you need to go a beginners' yoga class that's taught by someone who understands what it's like to be inflexible and has the right props on hand to help you out. That teacher needs to understand what it's like to be inflexible both physically and psychologically. Working with the right teacher will make all the difference – because you'll feel seen, supported, held and listened to. Plus the teacher will be able to give you the right modifications for your body.

For example, a key element of flexibility is our ability to move our pelvis – to tilt it forward or to hinge from the hips at a 90 degree angle. Most inflexible people can't do this, so when they go into a standing forward bend, downward dog or any seated posture the pelvis tilts backwards instead of forwards and the spine rounds. Without correct instruction, this doesn't help the body to open in any meaningful way and it can put pressure on the spine.

A skilled teacher will notice that your pelvis is tilting the wrong way and will help you modify the posture for your flexibility level – although different yoga styles approach working with inflexible students in different ways. In Ashtanga Yoga a patient and skilled teacher will ask you to keep your knees bent when you are doing

Downward Dog and forward bends, only taking you through small numbers of the standing poses until the pelvis begins to get that movement. There's just no point in moving on to the seated postures before then.

Bikram Yoga is designed for beginners and teaches the first forward bend with bent knees for everyone – beginners and experienced people alike. Plus the heat helps soften the body and the mind so it feels easier to bend.

Iyengar Yoga is tightly focused on alignment and uses copious props to ensure everybody is maintaining the alignment of the posture within their range of flexibility and strength. This can be very useful for beginners – it was the first kind of yoga I ever did, when I attended a ten week course.

Other alignment-based styles and teachers can also be very helpful in those early days of discovering your body and releasing years of tension.

The one style that may not be suitable for inflexible beginners is Vinyasa Flow. Of course, it depends entirely on the teacher and the pace of the class but in general Vinyasa Flow classes move faster, have less alignment-based instruction and don't use props. This means that people who are inflexible will move in ways that re-enforce their tightness rather than open it.

I teach Vinyasa Flow classes with usually around 15 people. I do give more alignment instructions and take time to initially break down poses before moving toward a faster flow. However, when I have a new person in class who can't bend in certain ways, I'll often structure the entire class around where their body is so they can have the right experience for their level. It's not detrimental to other people in the class who might be more bendy, but if I taught a fast-flow with certain postures it might be detrimental to the inflexible person.

This is why finding the right teacher is paramount. Ideally, sign up for a beginners' course where everyone else on the course is also brand new and the teacher takes more time to explain what's going on with the postures, working with each individual student so they know what's going on with their body and how they might need to modify postures along the way.

No matter what your fears and worries, there is no person that yoga is better for than the inflexible person. Releasing your body is an extraordinary experience. We get so used to living within a prison of tightness, it can feel liberating the first time we touch our toes with ease or place our bellies on our thighs. Our everyday movements become easier too – small things like being able to do up our shoelaces with ease or turn our head to reverse out of the driveway. Who doesn't want to be able to do that?

If inflexibility has been holding you back – ask yourself, what's the real reason that I don't want to go to class? Being inflexible is no excuse for not practicing yoga – yoga is *designed* for the inflexible.

I haven't got enough time to practice yoga

Of all the excuses that get bandied around for not practicing yoga, this one can be the easiest to counteract and, paradoxically, also the hardest to counteract.

When someone says 'I haven't got enough time to practice yoga', what they're really saying is 'Yoga is not a priority in my life'.

That's the honest statement, because there is *always* time for those things we value. We make time, even if we have to wring it out of our day.

If I counter their excuse with, 'There's always time in our day for the things we value' – the person I'm speaking to will often become defensive and start listing all the reasons why they really don't have time to practice yoga.

They work 60 hours per week on-call and travel often.

They work, as well as having young children and a partner.

They're training for a marathon already plus working a full-time job.

When those defensive patterns kick in, I know I'm talking to the person's ego. There's some part of the person's ego invested in holding up the status quo; that *believes* there's no time for yoga.

So I ask:

'Do you want to practice yoga? Do you want to go to class?'

Well yes, but...

'No, no buts,' I say, before asking again:

'Do you want to practice yoga? Do you want to go to class?'

I ask until the person can soften and open up to the question, responding with a whole-hearted yes. Now they've let go of ego (that which defends and holds against the moment) and I can speak to the deeper part of them.

If this is true, if you do want to go to yoga classes – given all the restraints of your life – *how* can you make it happen? What creative response could you come up with that would find a solution to all the busyness?

Now, instead of starting with not enough time and defending it, we've started with opening up to possibility and looking for solutions. It's a completely different mindset and it's coming from a different place. There's a different feeling to it.

Solution-finding feels different. It's about juggling, prioritising and figuring things out.

If you're a busy executive working crazy hours, where can you claim some free time of your own? What about doing a 45 minute lunchtime class twice a week and eating at your desk on those days? What about starting work earlier, finishing later, or just generally working more efficiently?

If you're a busy parent, can you claim one hour a week of your own? Can the other parent, a family member or a friend look after the children while you go and take a class? Could you find a Parent

& Bubs' class? Could you buy a great DVD and practice while the children sleep or when they're at playgroup or school?

If you're working on an oil rig six weeks on/six weeks off, can you practice at class three times a week while off the rig and then commit to three times a week for 15 minutes of home practice when you're back on the rig?

Often, as we start to explore our lives with a willingness to find a solution, unexpected ideas pop into our heads. We start to see the gaps rather than the obstacles.

Again, this very practice *is* Yoga. Just as we learn in class to shift from identifying with our thoughts and instead focus on the gaps between our thoughts, so too in solution-based living we shift from identifying with the obstacles to living in the gaps.

It often helps to do this exercise with a friend – preferably one who already goes to yoga class or has a home yoga practice. You need someone who is compassionate and can listen well – someone who can ask you, 'Okay, what else could you do? What else?' They're not there to give you solutions, but to prompt you to uncover your own answers. Just like a great yoga teacher...

Once you've established that 'having no time' is just another limitation in the mind, you may uncover a different reason why you're reluctant to try yoga. The time might be available to go to class, but you're still resisting going to yoga. This is common. Often the surface reason for not making it to class is not the real reason.

'I'd love to go to yoga.' 'Why don't you?'

'I don't have enough time.' 'Could you rearrange your life in some way?'

'Oh – yeah I could.' 'So you *can* go to yoga.'

'Yes but...'

That's what you want to look out for – that sense of '*yes, but*'. Any time a '*yes, but*' comes up, you know there's another layer of resistance to explore.

'BUT *I'm afraid of not knowing what to do.*'

'BUT *I'm afraid that people will laugh at me.*'

'BUT *I'm afraid of looking silly.*'

All of these reasons are perfectly okay. It's okay to feel like this. It's human to feel like this. That you feel like this is not the issue. The only issue is *how* you respond to these feelings.

Do you let them stop you from doing something you want to do on a deeper level? Or do you compassionately acknowledge these feelings and take action anyway?

That's training yourself to shift from being constrained by your mind, to acting from a place of courage and willingness. Yes, you know it, that's Yoga.

So if you're one of those people who have been meaning to try yoga for the longest time, but just doesn't have the time to do so... start with opening to a solution-oriented mindset. Figure out how you could make time, and then see if the reluctance is still there. If it is, then there is clearly a block getting in the way.

How do you figure out what that block might be? You don't need to. Oh you can figure it out if you like – root it out, let it go – or, you could just go to class. No matter what, even if you don't feel like it. Because you know a part of you wants to – otherwise you wouldn't be reading this book.

Feel the reluctance and go anyway. See what happens when you do that. Just... see...

I'm too old to practice yoga

No, you are not.
You are *not* too old to practice yoga.

You are *never* too old to practice yoga, ever. It could be your last day on earth, you might be 101, and you wouldn't be too old to learn how to breathe with awareness.

That said, it's also important that you find the right yoga for you and that can be far more challenging when you are older. It is true that there is less yoga on offer that's targeted specifically for older people. But this just means that you have to be more resourceful and determined to make yoga happen for you.

You may need to be downright tenacious. Finding yoga for older people might mean that you *demand* yoga for older people. You may need to call your local yoga teacher or yoga studio and have a good chat to them about who you are and what you want. Guaranteed, if there's one older person who wants to practice yoga, there are many more.

This isn't to suggest that older people need different yoga from younger people, just that the demands and realities of your body are likely to be different from a 20 year old. That said, there's not much difference between a stiff 20 year old and a spritely 80 year old who has stayed active his or her entire life – except that the 80 year old will likely find yoga easier!

Age is irrelevant when it comes to one's ability to do yoga. If you've been practicing yoga since you were a teenager, the kind of yoga you can do will be very different from someone who has only taken yoga up in their eighties. If you've always stayed fit and active – maybe you were a champion ballroom dancer – you might be in your seventies and be more than capable of dropping into a regular yoga class at the local studio.

Each and every case will be different. But as with all the other misconceptions about yoga, the first important step is to banish the limitation – 'I'm too old for yoga' – and replace it with possibility – 'There is a yoga out there that's right for me'.

Now you've got a possibility firmly established, you'll need to act on it and what that looks like will depend on many variables. How old you are. How active you are. What kind of living situation you're in – independent, supported, rest-home, hospital. The kind of community you live in – village, small town, big town, city. Your financial resources and your general resourcefulness.

For example, if you're living in a retirement village, it's likely you can make a request to the person who organises activities and ask them to organise yoga classes. You may need to get a few other residents on board to prove demand, but, with some cajoling, you can get the yoga brought to you.

If you haven't yet retired but are afraid of turning up to a yoga class filled with lithe young things, you need to do some research and find a class geared toward older people or a more gentle form of yoga. In a city, this shouldn't be difficult because of the sheer scope of yoga available. However, if you're in a small town, there might only be a couple of yoga teachers offering classes. Then you may need to meet with one and see if they offer a class that might be suitable for you or if they would be interested in starting one.

If you have sufficient financial resources, a good option is a one-on-one yoga class with an experienced teacher. The class would be totally tailored to you and, in time, you may find you're ready to join a general class.

Or, you could always get a small group of friends together of a similar age or physical aptitude and hire a teacher for small group yoga. It doesn't cost nearly as much as a one-on-one session, the yoga teacher would come to you and again the class can be tailored to suit the needs of your group.

So if you believe that you're too old to practice yoga, ask your-self: 'Am I really too old or is there something else at play here?' Because, just like all the other misconceptions we've looked at, blaming your age is a game of the ego. It's just a surface reason designed to keep you safe and secure and within your limits. Dig deeper and you're likely to discover that just like most people, you're afraid of looking silly, you're afraid of the unknown, and you're afraid of being uncomfortable. You're afraid, full-stop.

At this point you need to ask yourself: 'Do I want to live in fear or do I want to go to yoga class?' Taking the necessary steps to go to class means facing those fears, it means dropping the *'yes, but'* and shifting to a *'yes, and'*.

'I'm afraid of looking silly, *and* I'm going to call about that gentle yoga class I saw advertised in the local paper.'

Yoga is perfect for older people – in so many ways. Unfortunately there's not enough of it on offer that's specifically targeted at older people. But like everything else, it's a demand economy. There's a glut of yoga teachers out there right now struggling to make ends meet. If enough older people started demanding classes tailored specifically for their needs, some of those more astute yoga teachers would realise a great opportunity and jump on it.

Plus there's a wave of yoga teachers from the 1950s and 1960s who are now hitting *their* 50s and 60s and way beyond. Iyengar taught right into his nineties. An older yoga teacher generally has greater awareness of the needs of older yoga students. Who knows, we could be entering an Age of Golden Oldies Yoga.

But first, the most important thing you need to do is establish the possibility of yoga in your mind and then take the next steps to find the right class for you. Don't forget that yoga isn't just asana – it's also meditation, pranayama, chanting and Karma Yoga. You may discover that you adore chanting and are a natural-born Bhakti Yogi.* If you have limited physical mobility, you may discover that pranayama brings a new vibrancy to your life.

The key is to get out there and try things even if getting out there means surfing the Internet – or asking someone else to surf the Internet with you, and see what you can discover about yoga. Go to the library. Read a book. Talk to yoga-loving friends.

You are never too old to start yoga – ever.

---

* See the chapter on *'The four paths of yoga'*.

Real men don't do yoga

This is an odd misconception when you consider that Yoga's Indian roots are largely masculine. Yet the advent of yoga in the West has been dominated by female students since the 1970s.

It's a far cry from the 1920s and 1930s when Indra Devi travelled to India and had to persuade Krishnamacharya to take her on as a student. Now, yoga media is dominated by images of women practicing yoga. If men are shown, they're invariably wearing very little and showcasing enviable physiques. It's a double-whammy of intimidation for your average guy. First he's got to show up at a yoga class knowing he'll be in a guaranteed minority and possibly the only man in the room. Second, if there are any other men, they're likely to be seasoned practitioners who could double as models for the cover of Men's Fitness.

I'd be intimidated too!

But like all of the other reasons we don't show up to class, this one is another flimsy mind game masquerading as the truth. The fact is, men do practice yoga – always have and always will. Real men (whatever that means) most definitely practice yoga. In fact, the kind of courage it takes to show up to a predominately female class knowing that brute strength can't carry you through yoga is what *makes* a real man.

Men do find yoga more tough. They're less likely to be former dancers or gymnasts – as many of the poster yoga models often are. If they are fit and strong, they often find this works against them because they've become muscle-bound and can't get into the postures without some honed and precise alignment instruction.

If you're a man – and likely you are because you're reading this chapter – and you want to practice yoga but are intimidated by the all-woman vibe, consider finding a male teacher. They can be more difficult to find but that doesn't mean they aren't out there. A male yoga teacher isn't necessarily going to be a great yoga teacher, or a great yoga teacher for you, but initially having a male teacher may make you feel more comfortable going to class. In some towns, you may even find a men-only class, designed to encourage men to start yoga.

If you're male, you are likely to be tighter, so the chapter on flexibility may also apply to you. It's really important that you find a skilled teacher who can start you on good yoga habits. It is possible to injure yourself practicing yoga – especially if you're used to trying hard to be the best at what you do. Some postures aren't designed for beginners, even though you'll find them in classes aimed at beginners. For example, misalignment in Sun Salutations can stress lower backs and shoulders.

If you've got the financial means, I'd suggest booking a few sessions with a highly recommended one-on-one yoga teacher and finding out what your range of movement is like and what you need to be mindful of in a general yoga class.

For example, how does your pelvis move? Can you hinge forward at the hips? Or does forward movement result in a stuck pelvis and rounded spine?

How do your shoulders move? Do you have enough openness through the shoulders to lift your arms straight above your head while keeping the shoulders down and away from the ears? If not, how does that affect your Downward Dog? Are you putting pressure on your shoulder joints because they're not open enough yet to correctly align the posture?

In a general class, while a good yoga teacher will notice your alignment and attempt to help you find your way into the postures based on your current range of movement, this degree of attention can be difficult in a full class. Plus, for the new guy, it can make him feel like he's getting singled out for doing it wrong. Nobody wants to feel like that. A one-on-one session removes the audience and increases the dialogue. You can ask questions and make sure you understand how your body moves, how it needs to move and how to move it to encourage it to open up gracefully.

You could also get a couple of mates together to do a small group class. If you want to try yoga, it's guaranteed some of your friends want to as well. Hiring a teacher to teach you once a week until you get the hang of the basics will provide a solid foundation for attending class and for keeping your body safe and well.

There are many well-known male teachers – it's noticeable that the well-known Indian teachers (Pattabhi Jois, Iyengar, T.K. Desikachar, Krishnamacharya) are all male. All of the well-known Swamis who came to the West are male too – for example Yogi Bhajan, Swami Satyananda and Swami Sivananda. It's only when yoga made that leap from East to West that women teachers became the norm. Why? One reason might be that when yoga arrived from the East, it was mostly gentle, esoteric and taught by women in one-piece leotards on TV during the day. Everything screamed feminine.

Don't let this put you off.

Find a male friend who is into yoga and get him to take you to class. If you don't have a male friend who's going to class, find a female friend who is doing it – guaranteed you've got one of those. Observe how the thought of going to yoga class makes you feel – what thoughts come up? Are those thoughts true? Are you going to let those thoughts stand in the way of you and yoga?

Yes, you will be out of your comfort zone.

Yes, you will probably suck at yoga (when you start).

Yes, you will be asked to do weird things.

Yes, your body likely won't cooperate.

Yes, you will look silly.

But nobody else cares. Nobody else is watching – they're all too busy focusing on their own practice and if they are watching... it sounds like they *need* to focus on their own practice.

It takes great courage to go against the perceived social norm – but remember that it is only the perceived social norm in your country. Many sports stars practice yoga for the edge it gives them in performance. In the 21st century there is nothing weird or soft about practicing yoga. Yoga will challenge you more than anything else you've ever done and what better way to really test your worth as a man?

I'm too large to practice yoga

It's challenging to walk into a yoga class for the first time if you're bigger than the average yoga model. But most of us are. While you may feel like you're in a minority, you're not – there are way bigger people out there who've been too intimidated to try yoga. You're likely the vanguard, determined to give it a go even though you're worried about your size.

Not only do you have to contend with the usual intimidating factors of attending a yoga class for the first time, but you also have to hope you get a compassionate, skilled and experienced yoga teacher. If you don't – it's not your fault. Don't blame the yoga – just find another class.

Because the thing about yoga postures is that they are different for every body – literally. We all have different proportions and that can change the way we look in the postures and also what's possible for us to do in the postures too.

I have long arms, which makes bound twists easier. I can reach my foot with my hand by wrapping it around my body; not because I'm more flexible than the person beside me, but because I have a longer reach.

Bigger body parts make the postures different too – bigger breasts for example get in the way of lunges, as can round bellies. Weight-bearing postures become more difficult when you've simply got more weight to bear. You're doing more work than the rest of the class. This is why having the right teacher is really important if you're a larger student. They simply have to know more.

So know this – you're never too large to practice yoga. There's always a yoga that's perfect for you. The trick is to find it. Just like a man may feel more comfortable initially going to a male teacher, sometimes finding a larger teacher can make sense. They understand how bigger bodies move in class and they know how to cue for it. It doesn't mean you always have to have a teacher who is bigger – just that it can be helpful when you start so you can learn how to work with your body in the postures. Where do large breasts go in lunges?

If you're living in a small town, you may have far less choice of yoga, which makes it more difficult to find the right teacher. Fortunately, there's the Internet. Anna Guest-Jelley of Curvy Yoga is one larger yoga teacher who has done a great job creating a community of larger yogis. She's helped to bust (excuse the pun) the stereotype of yoga students as young slim things and also champions the education of regular yoga teachers in yoga for bigger bodies.

If you want to start yoga but you're intimidated because you feel like you're too big – get online and look up bigger yogis. Look at photos and videos to see what's possible. Find videos. Read articles and make comments. Find the community that's already out there and you will realise that there are heaps of people who feel exactly the same way you do, many of whom have gone on to find yoga and make it their own.

A big part of the yoga journey is how we shift from identifying with our bodies as ourselves to identifying ourselves as something deeper and more eternal than our bodies. This shift in identification can help us to accept ourselves as we are – regardless of what that is. Just because we're bigger, doesn't mean we have to be any other way. Sometimes bigger people go to yoga because they've heard it's great for weight loss. But not everyone who is bigger needs or wants to lose weight. Coming into a deeper acceptance of

Self is one of the great gifts of yoga – recommended for everyone, not just those who think they're bigger than everyone else.

Will yoga help you lose weight? It might. It all depends on what your natural constitution is, what your lifestyle is like, how often you practice and what kind of yoga you're doing.

It also depends on why you're bigger. Some people carry extra weight as a defence mechanism, as a way to hide. If you're practicing yoga consistently, you may slowly release the need for that defence mechanism and that extra weight might melt away.

Make no mistake, whilst yoga is a journey to the true self which means shifting away from identifying with the body, the yoga industry is no different from any other body-obsessed industry (like the fashion industry). It can be cruel and unkind and unintentionally or subconsciously promote fixed ideas about bodies, weight and fat.

Don't go looking to the yoga industry for enlightened ideas on weight. That said, individual yoga teachers are different. Some of them will understand that we are not our bodies and that we are perfect just as we are. These teachers will embrace you with compassion and acceptance whilst encouraging you to be compassionate and accepting of yourself.

Those are the yoga teachers you want to find and the classes you want to go to. The challenges you face starting yoga are more difficult than a slender student. Not only do you have to figure out how to adjust the postures for your size, but you are also confronting more psychological challenges, plus dealing with the general prejudice you may face in going to class. Simply acknowledging: 'Yeah, this is tough' is useful. It's seeing reality as it is, and steeling yourself for the action that is required.

Is it the physical aspect of dealing with your body on the mat?

Is it the social aspect of dealing with other people's attitudes (which can be really supportive or subtly judgemental)?

Is it your own psychological issues around body and weight?

Once you've worked out what's going to be the toughest thing for you, then you've got a clearer idea of the kind of support you need to embark on this journey.

If the social aspect is going to be difficult, can you find a friend to buddy up with you through the process? Can you find other larger yogis online to cheerlead you on?

If the body on the mat is going to be difficult, can you do a one-on-one session with a skilled teacher who can teach you how to modify common postures for your body?

If it's your own psychological issues around body and weight, can you journal through it? Or talk to a compassionate friend? Or work with a therapist?

Acknowledging what's going to be tough and then finding strategies to deal with that toughness before you start class is one way to help keep you on track. If you have these strategies in place you're more likely to go to class and stick with it.

Most of all, remember that Yoga is a personal practice that meets us wherever we are, whether we are large or not. If the class or teacher you go to makes you feel bad about yourself, there's nothing wrong with you. Find a different teacher or class. Keep trying classes until you find one that is safe and comfortable, where you can explore your body and mind while feeling supported.

Anyone can practice yoga – and that includes you, no matter what your size.

I've got a physical limitation or disability so can't practice yoga

Now surely if you're a quadriplegic you can't practice yoga right? I mean, how are you going to move anything, let alone do a posture!

Wrong.

Even if you're a quadriplegic you can still practice yoga.

Matthew Sanford, while not a quadriplegic, is an example of someone who has dedicated their life to yoga despite their disability. Matthew is in a wheelchair and paralysed from the waist down. He wrote a book called *Waking* about his experience – he was in a car accident at age 13, meet a yoga teacher in his early twenties, worked with that yoga teacher and eventually became a yoga teacher himself. I urge you to get your hands on a copy of his book and read it.*

His story will motivate and inspire you far more than I, as an able-bodied person, ever can. Matthew shows what is possible when you focus on the principles of yoga rather than the postures of yoga because that is the key distinction. Remember, yoga is NOT the postures – the postures are a tool that we use to practice yoga – at its essence, yoga is a state of being. Meditation and pranayama are also tools we use to practice yoga, and both of those can be more accessible if your mobility is limited in any way.

Of course Matthew Sanford is not the only person who has sustained a serious yoga practice despite serious limitations, whether real or perceived. There are thousands of people out there who have discovered yoga despite multiple sclerosis (MS), cerebral palsy, arthritis, or amputations. Whatever you're experiencing in your own life, try a google search on whatever it is "+ yoga". You'll be amazed at what you discover.

However, if you have a serious physical limitation it will be more difficult for you to find the right yoga teacher and class for you. It may take more determination and grit to show up and persevere. More will be asked of you.

The first step is to set a clear intention: 'I will find the perfect yoga teacher for me.'

---

* matthewsanford.com

The second step is to research your local area and find that teacher – see the chapter on finding a good yoga teacher for tips on how to do that.

You may not be able to go into a general yoga class, but depending on your range of mobility and ease of movement, you may be able to join a beginners' class or course. However, it's likely that the best way for you to learn yoga will be one-on-one with an experienced and skilled teacher or someone who is specifically trained in yoga therapy.

It usually costs more money to do a one-on-one session, although if you've got the right insurance it may come under some kind of therapy or healthcare costs. Plus, when you work one-on-one, the practice is more intense, as is the relationship with the teacher. More will be asked of you because you're the only one that they're working with in that moment. There's no drifting off in the middle of practice!

Plus, to get the full benefit out of your sessions, you need to practice at home. You need to take what you've learned – even if it's only one small breath technique – and do it by yourself. That takes courage and determination.

Your experience of yoga may be more frustrating or painful too. It depends on what kind of physical limitation you're experiencing, but you may struggle to do what's asked of you and face a much steeper learning curve. You may find that as you learn to develop a new and deeper relationship with your body you will become aware of new sensations which may not always be pleasant – at least, not at first.

In many ways you're a pioneer, going deep into the mind/body connection where few people have gone before. Your teacher will be able to guide you, but they won't know what it's like for you – unless they share the same kind of physical limitation. If you are really fortunate, you may be able to attend Matthews' classes!

Because your experience will be different from your teacher's experience, the two of you will be learning together. Much of what you do might be trial and error so your teacher will need feedback and in some ways, you'll be teaching him or her just as much.

The good news is that regular practice of yoga may help to improve your physical condition in some way. Yoga is no miracle cure and if you're in a wheelchair, it's unlikely you'll be able to walk again. (Although it has been known to happen. Don't discount anything.)

However, you may begin to experience your body in a different way and some symptoms may ease. There have been cases of people with MS who've gone into remission with regular yoga practice.

Garth McLean, a senior Iyengar teacher with MS has written about his experience of yoga and MS on his website. I'd recommend reading what he has to say.*

As with all the common misconceptions about yoga, the idea that we need to be in perfect physical condition to practice yoga is a myth. You don't have to be young or flexible, or female or thin or have all your limbs or even be able to move all your limbs. Yoga is a state of being and we use tools to practice that state of being.

The bottom line is, if you want to practice yoga you can find a way. Everything else is just an excuse, powered by fear. Make the commitment, find the way to make it work for you and enjoy the yoga. Yes, it will likely be harder for you, but that can also mean that the rewards are greater.

---

* yogarth.com/yoga-and-ms

2. COMMON QUESTIONS ABOUT YOGA

The language of yoga: common Sanskrit terms

One of the reasons that we sometimes find yoga intimidating is that it uses an entirely different language – Sanskrit.

Sanskrit is an ancient Indo-European language from which many Northern Indian languages are derived. It's considered one of the oldest languages in the world, older than Greek and even older than Latin. It is mostly used in scholarly and spiritual endeavours such as Hindu rituals, the study of Indian literature (much of which is written in Sanskrit) and of course, in Yoga. Sanskrit was never used for day to day conversation like English is.

Patanajali's *Yoga Sutras* were written in Sanskrit, as were most of the yogic texts that yoga looks to – which is why we continue to use Sanskrit in yoga classes today.

There is also a belief that each of the 50 letters in Sanskrit carries a different healing vibration or consciousness – hence the use of Sanskrit in chanting or Mantra Yoga. Thus when you use the correct Sanskrit name and pronunciation in class, you may be invoking a vibrational or energetic resonance as well. Of course, this relies on proper pronunciation and there's a good chance that much of the Sanskrit you hear in your average yoga class is sloppy and heavily accented.

Before you walk into your first class, it can help to have an understanding of the more common Sanskrit terms – it's a way of orientating yourself to the new and exciting terrain of Yoga. Here's some other common Sanskrit terms you may hear in class.

Asana

The word asana means 'seat' and has also come to mean 'posture', referring to the fact that postures are designed to make sitting in meditation easy and comfortable. As a result the word asana is also the suffix to every single yoga posture – so many of those big long Sanskrit words gliding off the yoga teacher's tongue aren't as long as they sound. It's just the constant addition of asana on the end that makes them seem longer, like Tadasana, Mountain Pose. Take off asana and you're left with Tada, which means Mountain. This understanding becomes useful when you get into the posture because if you reflect on the qualities of a mountain, you'll discover that Tadasana calls for those same qualities – a solid firm base rising up into the sky, still and strong.

In Sanskrit, the word asana is the plural for asan, which is the correct word for a singular yoga posture. However, asana in the yoga world has come to mean one posture and asanas many postures.

Astanga Yoga, Ashtanga Yoga, Astanga Vinyasa Yoga, Ashtanga Vinyasa Yoga

The difficult aspect about transliteration of a language into English is that there will sometimes be variances in how the English letters are used to depict the language. Such is the case with the 's' and 'sh' in Sanskrit. Correctly written, the 's' that sounds more like 'sh' has an apostrophe after it – s'. This makes As'tanga Yoga sound like Ashtanga Yoga but looks strange to English eyes. So often, the apostrophe was often dropped. However, that could lead to incorrect pronunciation as English eyes would read Astanga with no 'sh' sound. Hence the version that includes the 'sh', Ashtanga.

These two words are the same and have the same pronunciation, but are written differently depending on which system the writer has adopted. This also shows up in Savasana (Corpse Pose) which is pronounced Shavasana and can be written either way.

Compounding the confusion with the word Ashtanga Yoga is that it refers to two important aspects of Yoga – the first is Patanjali's codified system of the Eight Limbs of Yoga, called Ashtanga Yoga. The second is Krishnamacharya's codified system of asana postures, taught by Pattabhi Jois, called Ashtanga Vinyasa Yoga. That's quite a mouthful and people usually drop the Vinyasa when discussing Ashtanga Vinyasa Yoga – so you end up with Ashtanga (or Astanga). Common knowledge of this word is now the set sequences of postures that Pattabhi Jois taught, but Ashtanga Yoga actually refers to the entirety of Yoga as defined by Patanjali – the eight limbs of yoga.

Atman

The individual soul or essence of a person.

Aum (Om)

The most common and powerful Yogic mantra – Aum, as it's correctly written, is the sound of the Universe and deserved an entire chapter – see 'What are you Om about?'.

Bandha

A Bandha is a lock within the body – it's like the sluices on a canal that can block or release the flow of water. In class you may hear your teacher tossing about words like Mula Bandha and Uddiyana Bandha and have no idea what they're talking about. Ideally, any teacher using those terms in class and working with new people will make the effort to break them down and explain how to create the bandhas (locks) in the body. If the teacher doesn't do this within the first three or four classes, grab them after class and ask them to demonstrate for you, or in the case of Mula Bandha, give a good explanation. Over time bandhas will become more and more important in your practice, but when you first start yoga you want to keep things simple and not overwhelm yourself with too much information!

Drishti

This is your gaze point in each posture. However, it's one of those finer and more subtle aspects of practice which is often missed or glossed over in a busy yoga class. Each asana, as well as having particular alignment for the body, also has a particular place where you focus your gaze. As you breathe in the posture, you keep your eyes on that gaze point or drishti. Focusing the eyes like this helps to still the mind and bring you firmly into the posture, rather than having your eyes and attention wandering all over the room. If the teacher never mentions drishti, you can still make an effort in each posture to fix your eyes at one point and hold them there, even if you're not sure if it's the right place. In time, with good teachers and some research of your own, you will learn exactly where the gaze point is in all postures.

Mudra

While a bandha is mostly a lock that happens internally, a mudra is a seal of the body that happens externally, yet produces internal affects. Usually a mudra involves the hands, but it can also involve the entire body. A common mudra is placing the hands in a prayer position, pressing each palm against the other. This is Anjali Mudra.

Namaste

This is often a greeting or a way of saying goodbye. It means *the Divine in me honours the Divine in you*. Like anything, when the sounds are tossed out with no awareness of meaning, it's just sound. But when you take a moment to connect to the deepest part of yourself whilst reaching out to connect to the deepest part of the other person, and then say: "namaste", there is a different resonance or feeling sense. It's much easier to do and feel this at the end of class than it is at the beginning – after all, you've just spent an entire hour or 90 minutes focusing on connecting to the deeper part of youself.

Prana

Prana is life-force – that which animates all of life. It is our life energy. Like many aspects of yoga, first we know this intellectually and we may or may not 'believe' in it. Over time, with consistent practice, as we refine our ability to recognise the more subtle aspects of our mind/body, you can feel prana within – where it's flowing, where it's blocked, where it needs to move. A good yoga teacher will also be able to see this in their students – they'll see where prana is weak or blocked and be able to give you specific practices to help prana flow.

Pranayama

These are specific exercises that work with the breath. Prana or life-force, comes into the body with the breath and we move it around our bodies with breath – the two are intimately linked, although they are not one and the same. So when we work with our breath, we are also working consciously with prana. This can be power-ful and older more experienced teachers like Iyengar and Pattabhi Jois have always been cautious about how and when one teaches pranayama to students. Much of what we do in our yoga practice – our asana practice – is to strengthen the body's ability to hold a greater 'charge'. We're increasing our ability to hold more life-force. Pranayama can increase the amount of life force flowing in our bodies and if we haven't increased our ability to safely handle these higher levels, we can literally blow a fuse. So pranayama isn't merely playing with the breath, it's working directly with our life force.

Shavasana

This is the final posture in every yoga class – Dead Man's Pose or Corpse Pose. You lie down flat on your back with your eyes closed, palms extended down by the hips and facing up to the ceiling, and feet flopping out sideways about hip width apart. That's it. You just lie there.

Ironically, this can be the most difficult posture for many people. They can't close their eyes, they twitch about, they fidget, they want to get up and run away... but it's also the most important posture you'll do. This is where your body/mind integrates everything that you've done in yoga class. All those poses and all that breathing stirs up prana, which in turn stirs up your nervous system. Lying in Shavasana is the body's chance to settle, release and return to a place of equilibrium.

Too many beginning students make the mistake of thinking that class is now over and this lying around lark doesn't matter. Unfortunately for them, they don't always have a good teacher who explains the significance of Shavasana, or encourages students to stay in Shavasana. Many teachers will cue the posture and then leave the room, letting students decide how long to stay before they jump up and attack the rest of their day. If that happens, challenge yourself to stay for five minutes or at least twenty breaths. Take your time and observe your body/mind as it settles into a new configuration.

Ujjayi

This is a type of pranayama, most commonly used in Ashtanga Vinyasa classes and their derivatives like Power Yoga and Vinyasa Flow.

Ujjayi breath is engaged by gently restricting the flow of air in the throat, creating resistance to the air as it flows in and out of your lungs. This slight resistance makes the breathing action stronger and louder, sounding somewhat like a far-off ocean as the breath comes in, and then goes out again.

Again, it's one of those things where the teacher will often assume knowledge. "Engage ujjayi breath!" comes the command, with no explanation at all of what this breath is or how to do it. In your first few classes, don't worry about it. You've got enough to think about it with all the new words and body positions and just breathing a regular deep breath. After a few classes, if there's still no explanation coming from the teacher, call them aside after class and ask for help.

Vinyasa

This word can denote a style of yoga – Vinyasa Flow Yoga – and it can also be shorthand for a short sequence of postures – take a Vinyasa. The word itself means *to place in a special way,* and it's generally translated as breath-led movement. First one breathes, and then one allows the breath to move the body. An example of a common vinyasa is Sun Salutations. This is both Vinyasa Flow Yoga and a vinyasa. But a 'vinyasa' can be any sequence where the breath links two or more postures together. If the teacher is telling you to take a vinyasa, ideally they will have made it clear which particular postures they want you to include in this vinyasa, otherwise it's just sloppy teaching.

Yoga

The most common term of them all – Yoga is generally translated as union or to yoke. It's about bringing two things together. At its most esoteric level it's the union of the ego self with the eternal Self – or the dissolving of any sense of separate Self into All that Is. For your first yoga class, it's far more useful to think of Yoga as being union of body and mind, or union of breath and movement.

Taking time to tune into the nuances of the language can provide benefit. While it's easy just to hear long posture names like

Eka Pada Rajakapotasana as a mumble of sounds, if you take time to break out each syllable and extract its meaning, you can find clues to the shape of the posture. Eka is a number – the number one. 'Pada' means foot. 'Raja' means King. 'Kapota' means pigeon. And of course, you now know asana. Now, when you hear those sounds all running together you can start to pick out the different syllables and put them together, hearing One Foot King Pigeon Pose. From that, it's likely that there's going to be one foot involved in the posture somewhere...

It also means whenever you hear a posture that has Eka or Pada in it you know it's something to do with one and something to do with the foot. Simply by paying attention and tuning into the different syllables, you'll discover it's easy to pick up Sanskrit.

This shifts your experience of Sanskrit from just a wall of sound into something that translates the different aspects of Yoga to you.

What are the benefits of yoga practice?

I fumble when people ask me this question, or when they ask: "What's yoga going to do for me?" I pause and stare at them and wonder; *'where on earth do I start?'* Yoga can turn you inside out. It can have a profound effect on your psyche, on your body, on the way you love, on the way you see the world, on the way you live your life. How can I possibly share what yoga can do for you? Somehow, saying "everything" just doesn't cut it.

So here, I attempt to outline some of the possible benefits of a regular yoga practice. These are not all of the benefits – just a few selected benefits that will affect most people.

1. Strength

I watch beginners walk into my yoga classes, including big, strong-looking rugby-type men and I watch when they can't hold their own body weight in Downward Dog. Go figure. I don't care how much weight you lift, I don't care how many sports you participate in, nothing will make you strong from the inside out the way that yoga does.

It builds a strength that you can use. Not a 'limited range of motion strength' like weight training, but an all-over-body kind of strength that is powered by prana (life force).

This is kind of strength that means when you need to hulk two metres of wood from A to B, you can do it, and do it without straining anything. You're strong, but you're also balanced and flexible.

This is the kind of strength that means when you walk down a dark street late at night that mugger looks twice at you because something about your stride says: "Don't mess with her."

Yoga doesn't just build muscle strength either, it builds strong lung capacity.

It builds strong bones. It builds strong connections between mind and body (but more on that later).

One major benefit of yoga – it will create and maintain usable, all-over body strength for daily living.

2. *Flexibility*

Yep, it's a given, yoga makes you more flexible. Not cirque du soleil flexible, although it could if you were to dedicate yourself to it and you had the right body type to start with – but the kind of flexibility that improves your day-to-day life.

Yoga means you can bend over and tie your shoelaces without straining anything. Yoga means you can look over your shoulder to reverse backwards down a 100 metre drive without wrenching your neck. Yoga means you can have a healthy range of movement in all your joints and so are far less likely to get arthritis. Yoga means that you can comfortably sit cross-legged.

Yoga means that when I accidentally lock myself out of the house, I can reach my bendy arm in through the cat flap and unlock the kitchen door from the inside.

If you're bitching and complaining about how tight your body is, or thinking, 'I can't do yoga because I'm not flexible' see the chapter, *'I'm not flexible enough to do yoga.'*

This flexibility extends to more than just the body, your mind becomes more flexible too. Many of us have a rigid way of thinking – we believe that life has to be a particular way, that we have to be a particular way, that other people have to be a particular way. This rigidity begins to soften as we practice yoga. We become more flexible in our outlook, we're more open and willing to take on other people's points of views and less restricted in our ways of thinking.

3. *Balance*

Yoga works on your balance in a very real way. Because we're constantly working our bodies and nervous systems in all kinds of ways throughout our yoga practice, our bodies become more adept at shifting from movement to movement, resulting in greater balance. It means I can stand on one leg in the slippery wet shower and extend the other leg out in front of me to shave my legs and it's easy and fun. I like testing my balance all the time – just for fun.

Having physical balance in life makes us feel more balanced in other ways too. You'll feel more mentally and emotionally balanced. But for now, let's just focus on physical balance.

Regular practice of yoga means that if you slip on ice walking down a hill you're more likely to catch yourself before your butt hits the pavement.

If you're worried about the cost of medical care or the long waiting list for hip-replacements, or of falling and no one finding you in time, a regular yoga practice will improve your balance and give you more confidence.

4. Rehabilitation

You know that dicky shoulder you've got, that banged up knee, that tweaky back? You are going to have that for the rest of your life and unless you do something about it now, it will only get worse, and worse and worse.

If I was able to completely reverse the effects of degenerative disc disease and rehabilitate the lumbar spinal fusion I had at age 16 – think of what you can do!

In time, regular practice helps to rehabilitate whatever injuries you've already got. Even better, it can help to sort out the reasons why you got that injury in the first place, meaning you're far less likely to reinjure yourself.

My spine gave me trouble because of tension I was holding in my back – largely psychological tensions. The amount of back pain I was experiencing receded as I dealt with that tension and let it go through the practice of yoga, becoming more relaxed and open in life.

Yoga isn't a magic bullet, but if you're dedicated, consistent and do the right yoga for you, it can work wonders on a beaten up body. There are hundreds and thousands of people who have rehabilitated seriously banged up bodies through consistent yoga practice.

5. Prevention

How'd you get that injury in the first place huh? I'll tell you one of the factors contributing to mine. I had horrendously tight hamstrings and hips, which constantly pulled my pelvis forward, creating pressure on my lower back and on my discs until one day that pressure got too much and... pop!

If I had started practicing yoga before that happened, I might never have needed that spinal fusion.

Yoga will prevent all those injuries and illnesses you are setting yourself up for right now because you're not treating your body like the precious vessel it is. If you play any kind of competitive sport and you're not already doing yoga... what are you thinking?

Especially if you are involved in anything that involves leaping and twisting off high things like snowboarding, skiing, dirt-biking or mountain biking. It will drop your injury rate and improve your recovery time.

Yoga is the perfect complement for anyone involved in competitive sport and body practice, like dance. Maybe you've got a physically intense job that's doing a number on your body, even something like hairdressing. Yoga can help support your body so it doesn't get so wrecked through the everyday wear and tear you put it through.

6. Internal systems

Yoga doesn't just work on the muscular-skeletal system, it also works on the circulatory system, the endocrine system, the digestive system, the cardiovascular system... yoga just works on your insides, full stop. It keeps the energy moving and everything working the way it should.

Yoga keeps your insides in tip top condition so that they can deal with everything before it gets to be a problem, and when healthcare costs and waiting lists are what they are... there's nothing better than a regular yoga practice to help keep you healthy.

It doesn't mean you won't ever get sick – people who do yoga regularly still get cancer and die – but it does mean you're giving your body the best possible chance at staying healthy for longer.

7. Awareness

It's hard to quantify this particular benefit, but let's just say that when you spend ninety minutes being aware of your breath and remembering to contract mula bandha at the appropriate time... you start to notice things.

You become much more aware, and you notice things that once upon a time would have passed you by because you were too busy thinking of that hot guy on the train yesterday.

Yep, yoga tunes you into to the subtle energy of life. Any latent psychic gifts that you may have are likely to start showing up. It's like you'd been driving around with egg on your windscreen and didn't even notice…. and now someone's cleaned it for you and you can see lines on the road you didn't know were there.

This is the beginning of the shift from thinking your thoughts to beginning to notice your thoughts. It's when you can catch yourself thinking something and wonder, 'Is that actually true?' when normally you would have just believed that thought and taken action without even noticing.

You may even start to notice that there are different voices in your head – there's the Critic, or the Hothead or the Cynic or the Depressive. You start to become aware of how these voices aren't really you and don't always have your best interests at heart. This is a huge shift in awareness.

8. Clarity

Take that wily monkey mind of yours and focus it on your breath, your body, and a drishti (gaze point) and you find it starts to calm down. Not so much jumping here, jumping there or thinking this, thinking that. The peace that you seek – that contentment you think the latest fashion or car or house or partner can bring you… it lives inside you, under that monkey mind.

Before you start yoga, your mind is like a wave pool, complete with random surfers and who knows what's going on under the surface of your pool? It's too churned up to see. After yoga, your mind is like a pond in a Japanese Zen garden, fish clearly visible, rocky bottom clearly visible. Suddenly you're perceiving and your mind has stilled.

That's clarity.

It takes time to cultivate, but it's a fantastic benefit of regular yoga practice. Even better, once you learn a few yogic tools – like alternate nostril breathing – in those moments when you don't feel clear, when you're all confused and don't know what's going on or what to do, you can take a moment, sit down and do your practice. Afterward, you'll find that everything seems more manageable and things have become clear again. You start to realise that you have the ability to shift your state of mind through practice.

9. Knowingness

This one is very similar to clarity – clarity refers to the state of your mind, clear and still like that Japanese Zen pool. Knowingness refers to what can be transmitted through the clarity – it's the bubble of inspiration floating up from deep within the pond. When your mind is like a wave pool, that bubble of inspiration is often lost or confused with all the mess of bubbles created by the over-active mind. But when all is clear... knowingness can be perceived and experienced.

Knowingness is not having to call a girlfriend and endlessly debate whether or not you should go out with that guy because you just... well... know.

This is great because no longer do you need to rely on external cues to know what to do (seeking to please parents, friends, family, society, that hot girl next door) No, now you know your own heart, your own truth, and you know what to do.

I love this. When I'm having a moment of doubt and confusion... I hit my yoga mat, leaving the question behind and always (sometimes even on the mat) the answer becomes clear.

So if you are confused, anxious, doubtful or afraid – yoga can help you.

10. Union

This is why we do yoga and is what it's really all about. Yoga means to yoke or unite. This can be interpreted as the union between mind and body via that breath, or the union between self and All that Is. When you do yoga, you break down your identification with ego-self, and you become aware of yourself as just one drop in a giant ocean of consciousness. No more separate and alone, but together and One.

And this rocks, because when you are part of the whole, how can you ever be alone again?

Yoga is coming home to Source, coming home to God, coming home to life.

It's one of those benefits that sneaks up on you. People don't expect to go and do a few yoga poses and feel at one with the Universe but you may discover that when you walk out of class, everything just feels right. Everything is okay, just as it is. Colours may be brighter. Food tastes better. Music sounds amazing. This is you beginning to surrender into life as it is. This is the beginning of union. This is yoga.

11. Joy

If none of the other reasons gets you onto a yoga mat... this reason may be the one that wins you over. When I do yoga and I see my body move in ways I never thought possible; experiencing my strength, my balance, my flexibility, my rehabilitated body, my more injury-proof body, my awareness, my wonderful internal systems, my clarity, my knowingness and finally Union... I feel joy.

It erupts out from within me and fills the room.

Traveling around this world in a body that is a pleasure to inhabit, that looks after me so well, that moves so well, that functions so well... it's pure joy!

And this feeds back, over and over again. I get joy from practicing yoga and expression of joy makes me want to do yoga. I celebrate my body. I am grateful to it. I am in awe of it.

Regular practice of yoga helps you to understand that joy isn't dependent upon external circumstances but something that bubbles up from the inside when we get everything else out of the way.

These are just some of the many benefits of yoga – just a taster really. But you don't need to know what the benefits of yoga are to get on the mat – you just need to show up and do your practice. You'll then start experiencing the benefits yourself – right from the very first day. You'll know. You'll feel it. And those benefits are going to keep you coming back, time after time after time.

How fit do I need to be?

Once up a time, people thought that yoga meant lying around on the floor like old ladies and doing a few stretches.

However, more and more, people are realising that yoga can be an intense physical experience – especially yoga like Bikram, Ashtanga, Power or Vinyasa Flow.

So how fit do you have to be to go to your first yoga class?

A better way to phrase that question is:

'I am not/somewhat/very fit, so which class should I start with?'

There's such a broad variety of yoga on offer that you can match the style, teacher or class with your current fitness level.

First, if there is a beginners' course offered by the studio or teacher you've decided to go to, I'd highly recommend starting with that, no matter what your fitness level. You could be a marathon runner, and it would be the right place to start. See, while a varying level of fitness is required for all yoga, yoga is not about fitness at all. A good beginners' course will give you a thorough grounding in the basic elements of yoga – like breath awareness – so you've got a firm foundation to build on.

If you know that you're really unfit – for example you get out of breath walking up a flight of stairs – I would suggest either starting with a gentler form of yoga – a beginners' course, a Hatha yoga class, Yin Yoga – or starting with Bikram Yoga, which is great for beginners, albeit super challenging.

If you're doing Bikram for the first time, realise that it's not about doing every posture, it's about staying connected to your breath and taking as many breaks as you need to. In my first Bikram class, I think I sat down and took a break for every second posture. That's okay – you build up your capacity to stay with postures over time and it happens faster than you think.

Paradoxically, Ashtanga can also be a good place to start if you're not that fit – and if you go to an experienced teacher who's leading Mysore-style classes. In Mysore, everyone practices at their own pace and goes as far in the sequence as the teacher deems they're ready for. This means if you're a new student, and you're not that fit, an experienced teacher will likely take you through Sun Salutation A in your first class – and that might be it, until class number two.

What I don't recommend as a non-fit beginner is signing up for a Power or Vinyasa Flow class – at least, not without talking to the teacher beforehand. Power or Vinyasa Flow classes move at pace and when you're both unfamiliar with the postures and not particularly fit, it is not only difficult to keep up, but there's more chance of injuring yourself.

If you talk to the teacher beforehand, and if they're a good teacher, they will let you know if the class is suitable for unfit beginners – because some Vinyasa Flow or Power classes will be. It comes down to the way they're taught.

So how fit do you need to be for yoga? It depends on the class and it depends on the teacher.

Assess how fit you are and find the yoga class that's perfect for you. If you're not sure, use the '*How to Find a Great Yoga Teacher*' chapter, and once you've got that teacher lined up, have a chat to them. They will be able to recommend the right class for you – even if it's with a different teacher. That's the thing about a great yoga teacher; they're not so interested in converting you to the kind of yoga they teach or collecting you for their yoga class. They're more interested in helping you meet your yoga needs – finding the perfect yoga class for where you are right now.

It doesn't matter how unfit you are – there is a yoga class out there that will suit you.

Will yoga keep me young forever?

It's the Holy Grail of modern life, the never-ending quest for the elusive fountain of youth. That potion, procedure or diet that promises to keep one looking and feeling young forever.

Pity the poor celebrity, faced with growing older in the glaring light of public scrutiny, forever surrounded by images of themselves as a younger, brighter star.

But it's not just celebrities that fight the ever-advancing march of time. Regular citizens like you and I pour millions of dollars into highly touted solutions in an attempt to slow the ageing process. Creams and lotions, potions and pills... there's always a scientific breakthrough around the corner complete with new technical terms and spiffy diagrams that show exactly how this miracle product will halt the ageing process and make you young again.

But does it all work?

A quick glance around at the folk you stand next to in the pharmacy queue, or sit next to in the beauty salon, or workout beside in the gym will give you a ready answer.

No.

Because if it worked, none of us would have wrinkles, would we? We'd look young forever. As the glossy women's magazines are keen to show us week after week, even celebrities age, wrinkle and sag (Brad Pitt – how could you!). Time halts for no woman, nor man.

Yet it *is* possible to stay young forever.

Sri K. Pattabhi Jois did it – still teaching yoga as he approached his nineties. Krishnamacharya succeeded. So too did Iyengar.

In fact, spend any time in yogic circles and you will notice that while yogis still have wrinkles and they still sag... there is a youth-fulness and vigor about them that belies their age.

Yes, Yoga keeps you young.

And it keeps you young in the only way that really counts – on the inside. Yet when you're young on the inside – young organs, young joints, young nervous system, young outlook – you also look younger on the outside. You glow from the inside out.

Because what does it mean to be young?

Does it mean that you have a smooth, wrinkle-free, expression-less face that hasn't changed in twenty years?

Or does it mean that you leap out of bed in the mornings excited about what adventures you might encounter today?

Does it mean that people mistake you for your daughter?

Or does it mean that you can get up on the mountain with your daughter and spend the week snowboarding?

Does finding the fountain of youth mean you never have to grow up and face the reality of life?

Or does finding the fountain of youth mean that you face the reality of life with childlike wonder?

This is what it really means to be young – it's the way you look at the world, it's the way your body moves, it's your willingness to embrace the new and step outside the comfort zone.

Yoga works on all these aspects of youthfulness – and more. Watch yogis practice and you can see that our bodies age not because the years roll on by, but because they become accustomed to the range of movement that we put them through.

I hear people talking about ageing all the time – attributing the passing of the years to the fact that they are getting stiffer, more rigid and closing down. They moan about the things they can no longer do because they're now older. While there is a grain of truth to this – a seventy year old yogi will be different from a twenty year old yogi. Much of what we attribute to ageing is merely the natural response to a body that is no longer put through a wide range of motion – and of course, because we can no longer easily do those motions we do less and it becomes a self-fulfilling prophecy.

Practicing yoga postures helps to reverse the ageing process by moving our joints through their full range of motion. We stretch, strengthen and balance every aspect of our body. Yoga is all about opening and expanding, not just our body but also our minds and our hearts. It's these two latter aspects that have much to do with the anti-ageing properties of yoga. We stay young in mind and young in heart because we're still open.

If you really want to know how 'old' you are – don't look at your birth date, nor even the number of grey hairs or wrinkles you have. Instead, see how bendy your spine is – in yoga, age is measured not in chronological years but with the saying:

"You're only as young as your spine."

This means when I started yoga back in my mid-twenties in order to fix the rigidity in my spine (I couldn't touch my toes, let alone my knees!) I was actually closer to 70 years old. Thank goodness I started yoga then. Now with my spine opening up, I figure I've reversed the ageing process so much I'm in my late teens again – at least, that's how old I feel!

Remember, our spine contains more movable parts than any other part of our body. It's connected to our pelvis, our legs, our arms and our head. When the spine gives way, it's often at one of those connection points, and the agony and stiffness carries through to the rest of our body. But when you can still bend forward with ease to put your shoes and socks on, bend sideways to retrieve a magazine off the ground or bend backwards to stare up at the stars – you're still youthful.

And no matter how old you are today, you are never too old to start yoga. The day you start yoga is the day you stop the hands of time ticking by. Many yogis, like Betty Eiler,* begin yoga late in life but still find the practice can completely change and open up their body. Betty says she learned to do Hanumanasana (splits) when she was 52 and Urdhva Dhanurasana (Wheel pose) at 55.

Beryl Bender Birch, a long-time yoga teacher and founder of Power Yoga back in the 1980s recently released a book called *Boomer Yoga*. In it, she confronts ageing from a yogic perspective – yes, the body will be different to when you're young, and old injuries may play up more, but you can still stay younger than your peers by regularly practicing yoga.

If the advancing years are making you reach for the potions and pills and you don't like to look too closely at yourself in the mirror anymore, if it feels like your body is beginning to betray you... now is the time to start yoga.

It's not a miracle worker.

You will still age and get wrinkles and grey hair.

But with yoga, you can keep your body in the best possible health. You can keep expanding your comfort zones and the range of movement possible for you. Like Betty, you may find yourself able to do a headstand or handstand even though you long ago passed 40, or 50 (or even 60!).

No matter how old you are right now, it's never too late to start yoga, and yoga will always keep you younger than you would have been without it. It won't just keep your body open and free, it will also keep your mind and heart open. If that's not a reason for a regular practice, I don't know what is!

---

* bettyeileryoga.com/background.html

Will yoga give me a great body?

We live in a culture obsessed with finding the perfect body. Many people start yoga for exactly that reason – although many people are also not sure if yoga will give them a 'good body'. The short answer is... yes, yoga will give you a 'great body'.

The more interesting answer is that as you practice yoga, your perception and understanding of what a 'great body' is will change.

Even more interesting – the concept that happiness is reliant upon creating specific circumstances (i.e. when I lose weight I'll be happy; when I win the lotto I'll be happy; when I find my perfect partner I'll be happy) is revealed to be an illusion.

What this means is that whether or not your body is 'good' ceases to matter, because you're happy and content anyway. But right now, those of you who are looking to begin an exercise practice that will improve the condition of your body don't care about that. Nope, you just want to know, is it worth investing time and money into yoga to get the body I want?

I'm here to tell you, yes it is. Absolutely. In fact, despite the fact that I do no other serious exercise and eat whatever I want... at 38 years of age I am in better shape than I have ever been. And it's all down to yoga.

Yoga will give you the very best body you could possibly have for your body type if you practice regularly. What your body type is will vary wildly though.

I can't put it any simpler than that. Here's how it works.

The practice of physical postures, or asana, works far more than just your muscles. It doesn't just lengthen and strengthen – although it does that super well. Yoga, because of its mindful attention to the breath amongst other things, works every single system in your body – it works your body from the inside out.

I don't want to list all the ways that yoga can improve your body based on what I've read, or even what other people have told me.

No, I'm only going to tell you what I have experienced myself, as I know these improvements to be 100% true and possible.

Here's what's happened to my body since I began to practice yoga regularly:

1. Regular practice of physical yoga means I maintain my ideal body weight with ease and no thought necessary – no dieting, no restrictions on food. I eat what I want when I want. In practice, because my system is more sensitive and I am more tuned in to what things really feel like, I don't want to eat crap food because it makes me feel like crap.

It's not about discipline – I just don't enjoy processed icky food anymore. Oh, I still love chocolate – in small doses. I love cheese. I enjoy a glass or two of wine. There is nothing I won't taste or sample, but I can feel when I have had enough and I stop there. When I do crave food, it's the good things in life – like asparagus, or zucchini, or salad. Yes, a salad craving has become normal for me!

2. Yoga has improved my lung capacity – yoga is not thought of as a cardio workout, but because you are mindfully breathing and taking long deep breaths your lung capacity will improve. Plus, if you practice pranayama, it will improve even more.

I notice my improved lung capacity when I'm walking up hills or climbing stairs. I can always breathe with ease, and it just feels like my body is able to extract oxygen from the air and get it to every cell in my body far more efficiently than it could when I was in my early twenties and working out on the treadmill. I would love to have my lung capacity tested, just to see the numbers on paper, but you know it yourself when you're breathing easy, and damn if it doesn't feel good.

3. Yoga has improved my flexibility – this is the obvious improvement from yoga. When you practice regularly, your body will open

up – and depending on how tight you are when you start, it might open up enormously.

When I first started, I couldn't sit on the floor with my legs out straight in front of me. In real life, this meant that I was unable to bend over to tie up my shoelaces. I had to find somewhere to sit and awkwardly hoist my foot up close enough to my body to reach. Not a good look when you're only 25! Now even small actions, like turning around to look behind me when I reverse the car, are graceful and easy.

4. Yoga has improved my balance. Balance ties in with strength and flexibility. In practice, it's hard to quantify what improved balance means in my day to day life. But I know it means I am far less likely to fall over and hurt myself – something that matters a lot as we age and our bones get more brittle. Plus if I feel like jumping up onto low walls and walking along them just for fun because I can, I have no qualms about it. And that's a cool thing.

5. Yoga supports my health – it's fantastic. How many sick days have I had in the last five years? I can't remember – maybe less than a handful. It's a standing joke in my household, when a bug comes through other people will be hit for three or maybe five days. I'll get the condensed version and feel a bit off colour for maybe six to twelve hours. Health is one of those intangible assets that we don't really notice or appreciate until it is gone, but it's definitely worth practicing yoga and building it up.

6. Yoga has made me strong – very, very strong. The beauty of yoga is that it works every single muscle in the body. Bicep curls may give you a large bicep but what about all the other little muscles in the arm?

Yoga strength is being able to hold yourself up in inversions and in arm balances. It's sitting deep in Warrior II for a long period of time and finding a place of grace and lift. It's coming into Warrior III and feeling like you're superman or superwoman.

It's not just strength of body either; it's strength of mind. Yoga teaches us to stay with our discomfort, to sit with our awful feelings. When you do this enough times, you begin to realise that discomfort and even pain do not touch the core of who you are.

It's possible to go within to a place of peace even while your feelings, thoughts or physical sensations are causing you discomfort. I've been fortunate in my life not to ever experience any physical violence, torture or even prolonged pain (beyond that of my spine and childbirth) but I imagine that if I ever needed to yoga would have given me the strength to endure. And that's a big thing.

7. Yoga means I can now hold a tune. At least, I can sing and feel good about doing it and I *think* I'm in tune. Yoga encompasses chanting, such as Kirtan. Kirtan is a call and response jam session with instruments and Sanskrit chants and it absolutely rocks. I added Kirtan to my practice in my early thirties, and I never thought I'd feel so damn good about opening my mouth and singing.

8. Yoga means I love my body, inside and out. As a hyper-critical, perfectionist teenager and young adult, I wanted the perfect body and worked damn hard to get it. In doing so, I was completely missing the fundamental truth that my body was already perfect. In fact, my body was an amazing feat of biology that was housing my soul and doing a great job in moving me from A to B. I had little appreciation for it at all!

Instead, if I looked in the mirror, my gaze would go to those bits I hated and I would obsess over what I could do to fix them. I mean – give me a break, talk about self-absorbed and narcissistic!

Now however, I have an immesne appreciation and wonder for my body – I feel so blessed. I can run, walk, jump, leap, twirl, and twist, sometimes I even feel like I could almost fly... if I could only find a superhero costume!

But seriously, my mindset has shifted and when I look in the mirror at myself now I grin. I appreciate what is there, because it won't be there forever. I will age and my body will change, and there may come a day when I struggle to make it to the bathroom. So today, when my body is 100% fit and fighting, damn it if I won't appreciate it and love it for the miracle that it is.

Of course, in shifting to this mind space where I love my body, I realise that it's not actually *having* a great body that we want. We just think it is.

What we truly want is to look in the mirror and feel awesome about ourselves. We want to be able to walk down the street with a bounce in our step and a glow on our faces. In our upside down way of seeing the world, we believe that we have to control our external circumstances in order to create this feeling and these thoughts inside of us.

But that's not true – and practicing yoga will help you to understand this. Practicing yoga will give you a good body, not just because it changes and reshapes your body (although it does do this).

Practicing yoga will give you a good body because it pierces your illusions and reveals that you already have a good body. In fact, you already have an excellent body. It's just waiting for you to see it, appreciate it and celebrate it.

And if you don't believe me, then get to a yoga class and see how your perception of your body shifts after regular practice. Let me know in a year or two if I was right.

Enjoy the yoga!

Is yoga a religion? Do I need to be spiritual?

Oh this is a tricky question and there's many ways to answer. One could write an entire book about this subject.

Let's start with a short answer; no, yoga is not a religion. You are not asked to believe anything, and neither are you asked to bow down before or worship a God or Gods.

No, you don't need to be spiritual – whatever that means. Let's take it to mean that you don't subscribe to any particular religion, but you feel like there is something greater than you in life. Perhaps something that sticks around after your body is gone – a soul if you like. You don't have to believe or know that. You can be agnostic and practice yoga. You can be religious and practice yoga. You can be spiritual and practice yoga, or not spiritual and practice yoga. It doesn't matter. Yoga doesn't ask anything of you when it comes to beliefs or ideas about God or the nature of life. Yoga will meet you where you are.

However, yoga does reference a concept of God, it does provide its own creation myths, and it does explain life as we know it. The difference between yoga and a religion is that yoga doesn't care if you believe the same things or not.

In fact, yoga would rather you didn't believe anything at all and instead did your own practice and saw where it took you and what you experienced. From that place of experiencing you might come to know some things – or not.

That means the longer answer is that with a dedicated yoga practice, you may find your understanding of your Self and of the world shifting and changing.

An even longer answer would examine the roots of yoga, which are primarily Hindu, and look at how that religion influenced yoga and the practice of yoga. Note too though that Hindu as one religion is only a recent phenomenon. That was how the British perceived the way Indians practiced religion.

In reality, Hinduism is a collection of a myriad of ways of worshipping God and life. It's from Hinduism that you find many of the Gods that influence yoga – such as Hanuman, the Monkey God. His name graces the full splits – Hanumanasana. Why?

Because as legend tells it, when Sita was stolen by Ravana, King of Lanka, her lover Ram sent his most loyal lieutenant to recover Sita. She'd been whisked away to the Kingdom of Lanka (Sri Lanka), and Hanuman had to leap from the tip of India to Sri Lanka to rescue her; that leap is the splits.

Do you have to believe in these Gods and legends to practice the splits?

Not at all – it's completely irrelevant. However, what's interesting about the overlay of Gods and legends on yoga practice is what the stories and characters can reveal about our own psychological journey and how that can relate to particular asana.*

Take Hanumanasana for example.

Physically opening into this posture requires a leap of faith because our innate tendency as we lower ourselves down into the splits is to grip and hold on because we're afraid of being torn in two. We don't feel supported and we don't know how we're going to hold ourselves safe in this posture.

Turning to the legend of Sita, Ram and Hanuman offers clues as to the psychological shift required to release into the posture. Hanuman had no fear – he had total faith. Hence the leap of faith. But he was also strong and steadfast. In this posture, accessing our own strength and ability to be steadfast helps us learn how to have the faith to let go. We learn which parts of the body need to be engaged – strong and steadfast – so we can have the courage to let go and release into the posture.

---

* Note that this approach to yoga is grounded in Tantra, as compared to just Hatha Yoga. All of this is described in more depth in the chapter on '*Yoga Philosophy, History and Concepts*'. Tantra is older than Hatha Yoga, and rather than a proscribed set of practices it is a philosophy that encompasses Hatha Yoga. According to Swami Akhandananda Saraswati, a Satyanandi Yogi, Tantra is the basis for yoga – it is the philosophy, and yoga is the practical application of that philosophy. Tantra's purpose is provide each of us with the exact practice we need to evolve consciously. For this reason, Tantra includes a wide variety of approaches to suit a wide variety of people.

Whether or not Hanuman ever existed becomes a moot point. The more interesting question is, can this story help my practice?

Much of yoga is like that. There are all these stories or ideas about the way the world works. You can ignore them all if you like and just focus on your breath and your practice. Or, you may find that these stories and ideas fascinate you and you read about them, learn about them and find ways to apply them to your practice.

One of my favourite stories from yoga is that of Shiva and Shakti. Shiva is male energy – the masculine. He's consciousness – the consciousness of the universe out of which all else arises. Shakti is female energy – the feminine. She is movement, energy or change. Shiva existed before all else, he's all there was.

In the story one of my teachers told (the Tantric scholar Christopher Tompkins), Shiva was doing his thing one day, that is, not much. Shiva just is – pure meditation one could say. But Shiva was bored; it was only him and only stillness; only purity. He wanted something else – the Other. So out of himself, Shiva created Shakti. She is the movement, the energy, the dance, the creation. It's as if Shiva was the ocean, still and endless, and Shakti is the wave, moving and appearing separate yet ultimately part of the whole.

When we sit in meditation and find stillness, with practice we may one day experience a place where we dissolve into everything else; where there is no separation between us and the other and where we recognise that All is One. This isn't because we've learned it or because we believe it, or even because we know it. This is because in that moment, we experienced it. We became All That Is. This is Shiva.

Yet nothing lasts forever and even in our meditation we will drift out of that state. We will have to stop meditating and stand up and go pick our children up from school, or head into that meeting ,or get dinner ready, or go off to sports practice. Now we have become Shakti (whether we're male or female). We are energy, movement and change. We are separate from the ocean, but still ultimately a part of it.

In this state of being, there is a deep surrender to the unfolding nature of life. Thoughts may have slowed down considerably. We are still in charge of ourselves – we're still making choices, yet there is also a deep abiding sense of rightness about everything. The choice we make is the only choice we could possibly make; yet it is still a choice. All internal conflict ceases and we are completely at peace.

These states of being can happen as a result of yoga practice – and not just to people who dedicate their entire life to yoga or disappear off to practice in a cave for years on end. There have been times – not many, and not for long – when I have experienced Shiva consciousness; where I ceased to exist as such and instead knew myself as All That Is. More common in my experience though is Shakti consciousness. This is when I feel like I am being danced. There is a deep surrender to the moment and it's crystal clear exactly what to do and say in each moment. It's like a light or current opens up both within and without and all I need do is step into that light or current.

The first few times I had these experiences, I knew nothing of yoga and had no way of putting them into context.

Later, as I began to learn more about yoga besides just asana, my understanding grew and I was able to conceptualise my experiences. Some would say conceptualising an experience is a step backwards but in our Western world, which is largely materialist and secular, experiences beyond the pale can be frightening and dislocating – no matter how blissful they are.

When I heard about Shiva and Shakti – although they're portrayed as Gods – my teacher explained what they meant metaphorically and psychologically, and I was able to relate them to my experiences. It deepened my understanding and helped me let go further into my yoga practice. I had a real sense of 'Oh, other people have been here before and they've shared their experiences through these stories and myths. This is known territory!' There was great comfort in that and also some excitement. It was like discovering another Planet Earth that one could explore.

In this way, the many myths and Gods of yoga have little to do with religion and everything to do with helping us understand the terrain of our psyche. This can be just as threatening to some religions – or at least, some people who practice some religions. Some fundamentalist Christians have been known to think that yoga practice invites the Devil into one's being. Metaphorically, I would suggest that the Devil is doubt. Practicing yoga will make you question yourself and what you believe, that much is true. Those questions can lead to doubts in whatever religion you ascribe to. However, it doesn't mean that your religion isn't true for you or that you need to abandon it or that you stop practicing yoga and be a Muslim, or a Jew or a Christian. In fact, yoga practice can enhance your experience of religion, whatever the religion is. Blind faith might crumble, but out of that can grow a deeper knowing of your God.

In your practice, it's up to you how much of the deeper philosophy and esoteric understandings you explore.

You may be content to just stay in the realm of physical postures or you might dive into the deeper understanding of yoga through legends, myth and ancients texts. This is the beauty of yoga – it is neither this nor that, but all and everything.

What are you OM about?

The number one thing that freaks out new yoga students is the thought of opening their mouth and making a vowel sound followed by a consonant in a room full of strangers.

Yes, the simple sound of 'OM' makes people want to run screaming from the room.

There are a few reasons for this – one is that aum (as it's correctly written) has a bad rap. It's weird, strange and the butt of all kinds of jokes.

Plus, making a sound like aum brings up all the fears we have about yoga being some strange cult or weird religion. A bunch of people sitting cross-legged and aumming out loud – when viewed from the outside – can look like brainwashing.

Add to this the fact that people are freaked out by how they might sound and the idea of aum becomes downright challenging. Very few people have made the sound aum before they come to a yoga class and they have no idea if they're going to sound like a dying cow or an ascending angel.

That fear – 'oh shit, what am I going to sound like' – shuts people down and ironically that is when they're more likely to sound like a dying cow, if they make any sound at all.

So what is aum and why do yoga teachers force us to sound it out at the beginning and/or end of classes? Some teachers even make us do it during class, in the middle of postures. What's with that!?

Aum is apparently the sound of the universe. That is, if you were to listen very, very, very closely and pay extra super duper attention you could *hear* the hum the universe makes as it goes about its business of expanding and growing into infinity…. you would hear aum. At least, that's what the yogis say. I haven't listened hard enough and I have never heard the universe aumming. That doesn't mean it isn't happening, though you don't have to believe me, just as I don't have to believe the yogis.

Remember, yoga is experiential.

However, we can refer back to some of the ancient texts to get some context on this sound aum.

Aum is mentioned in the first paragraph of *The Mandukya Upanishad*, which was written sometime around 800–500 BCE. This text explains both the concepts behind the sound and the symbol.

> *The syllable aum, which is the imperishable Brahman, is the universe. Whatsoever has existed, whatsoever exists, and whatsoever shall exist hereafter, is aum. And whatsoever transcends past, present, and future, that also is aum.* ~ The Upanishads: Breath of the Eternal by Swami Prabhavananda (translator) and Frederick Manchester (translator)

The text goes on to say:

> *Om is pure unitary consciousness, wherein awareness of the world and of multiplicity is completely obliterated. It is ineffable peace. It is the supreme good. It is One without a second. It is the Self. Know it alone! This Self, beyond all words, is the syllable aum.* ~ The Upanishads: Breath of the Eternal by Swami Prabhavananda (translator) and Frederick Manchester (translator)

In translation, chanting aum reminds us that we are all divine, as is everything around us – that everything which exists is connected through this divinity.

But there's more – aum also represents the four states of human consciousness, as seen by the yogis.

Vaishvanara is the first state of consciousness. It is our normal waking state, which is perceived through our five senses and naturally focused outward to material objects and the material world. The second state of consciousness, Taijasa, is dreaming sleep or the mental nature, which is focused inward to only the thoughts in the mind. This isn't just when we're asleep and dreaming, but can also refer to day dreaming states of being. The third state of consciousness, Prajna, is dreamless sleep or deep meditation.

The fourth state of consciousness is Turiya, and is the hardest to describe – so difficult that even *The Mandukya* calls it 'indescribable'. But that hasn't stopped other people from attempting to describe the indescribable. Turiya is a state of transcendence – actually THE state of transcendence or liberation, where the Self is united with Source and there is no longer any separation between Self and Source. This is liberation or self-realisation – the whole point of Yoga.

These states of consciousness become more apparent when you break aum down into its component sounds – A – U – M.

First you sound 'ahhhh like you're opening your mouth wide for the doctor, then 'oar' like paddle of a canoe and finally 'mm-mmm' like you've just eaten the yummiest ice-cream ever. Those three sounds roll into each other 'ahhhh...oar... mmmmm' and create the sound of aum.

Those are the three states of consciousness – Vaishvanara, outward focus on the material; Taijasa, dreaming sleep or inward mind focus; and Prajna, dreamless sleep or deep meditation. The fourth state, Turiya is found in the silence after the aum – where there is no sound, but there is an indescribable 'something'.

Each of the components also relates to a different chakra or energy centre in the body. 'A' is the root chakra, 'o' is the heart chakra and 'm' is the third eye chakra. The silence at the end is the crown chakra, which connects us to Universal Consciousness.

So as one sounds each part of the aum, your awareness and attention moves through the four states of consciousness and up through the body. First, full awareness is brought to the root chakra and you feel the sound of 'ahhhh' reverberating through the lower pelvis and groin. This is the world of the material.

Then the sound travels up the spine and you move in the heart chakra where 'oar' reverberates in the upper chest area. Now you're entering the dream states or inward focus of the mind. From here you move up the back of the neck and through the top palate of the mouth as you 'mmmm' and the energy rises up to the third eye. This is the state of dreamless sleep or deep meditation. Finally, as you sit in the silence afterward, you're in the crown chakra and the illusions that separate you from the Universe dissolve.

That's a real aum. Not just a sound made with the mouth, but an energetic experience in the body that opens and balances the chakras and moves you through the four states of consciousness.

Now *this* I have experienced and it's an incredible experience – especially if you're in a room with 20 or so other yogis also bringing full awareness to the energy of their bodies and moving up through their chakras.

Everything starts to tingle and it feels like the body gets lighter and the room gets lighter and a new dimension opens up. But don't take my word for it. Instead, open up to aum and give it a go yourself. Aum is one of those things that's really easy to do at home even if you've never gone to a yoga class in your life – all you have to do is get over yourself and how silly you might feel.

It's important to remember too that you're not singing the sound aum, but allowing the sound aum to move through you.

For those who are more scientifically-minded, sound vibration is a powerful force. Think of an opera singer hitting those high notes and breaking wine glasses. Vibration has an effect on matter – and we're all made of matter. Making sounds – specific sounds like aum – affects us in a profound manner.

Will you have to aum in your first yoga class? Maybe, maybe not. Many classes skip the aum completely – too weird and out there even for the teacher, or sometimes just not appropriate for that particular yoga class. You'll never hear aum in a Bikram Class and unlikely in a Hot Yoga Class. However, other classes don't just aum, they'll use other Sanskrit chants. Ashtanga classes have a specific chant they use to open and close class. Anusara opens and closes class with chanting while in classes like Satyananda you are most likely to aum at least a few times, you might even get an Aum Shanti chant.

If you really want to experience full-on chanting, find yourself a Kirtan session. It's not really a yoga class per se... it's a bunch of people coming together to get high and trip out on mantra; because that's exactly what happens.

At Kirtan, there'll be a few instruments, like a harmonium (a droning-style piano-like instrument), guitar, drums, shakers and maybe even a triangle. Someone at the front will call a chant – usually one or two lines at a time – and everyone else will respond. It will go back and forth like this, for perhaps ten or fifteen minutes, verbal chanting tennis, building up to a crescendo before dropping down into stillness again. Everyone will sit silently and let the vibrations wash over them and then do it all again – maybe four or five separate chants in a session. Of all the yoga I've ever done, this is the style most likely to induce a blissed out state of being. Although it's worth noting that this state of highness can be a distraction along the path. Like anything, we can get stuck here, addicted to the high and not moving onward to open in full liberation, another cul-de-sac on the road to enlightenment.

For now though, if blissing out after ninety minutes of chanting sounds like the scariest thing ever, just contemplate uttering three humble aums.

Try it by yourself at home, playing with the sound. See if you can bring the 'ahhh' up from the very pit of your belly, the deepest part of your being. See if you can expand the 'oar' out from your chest and make it as huge and wide and round as you can. Finally, take the 'mmmm' and lift it through the roof of your mouth and out of your third eye expanding in the universe to infinity. Then sit in the silence focusing your awareness on the crown chakra.

As you do this, notice where the energy or sound gets stuck – pay attention to all the chakras as you move the sound up from the root chakra, through the sacral chakra and navel chakra to your heart and up through the throat to the third eye chakra.

Aum is like a yogic diagnostic tool. The places where the sound gets stuck or the energy can't flow indicates areas of the body/mind/psyche that are blocked or shut down, which is exactly why aum freaks out some people – it reveals our insides. You can literally hear the person who's afraid to love, or the person who squeaks out the sound because they've never been able to speak up for themselves.

We don't like revealing ourselves in public and aum just feels too damn intimate to share with a bunch of strangers in a yoga class. The person who's comfortable doing a full-bodied, open and expressive aum is the person who's comfortable in their body, and comfortable opening up to others and expressing who they are.

That's what aum is all about – nothing more than opening to the sound of the universe, tuning your chakras and moving through all four states of consciousness. All you have to do is open your mouth and let a sound move through you.

Easy, right?

3. YOGA PHILOSOPHY, HISTORY & CONCEPTS

A brief history of yoga & lineages

I dove into research to write this chapter and I almost drowned... there is so much information about the history of Yoga – which stretches back thousands and thousands of years. As I'm not a historian nor a Sanskrit scholar, I had to ask myself – what is the most essential information here? What does someone brand new to yoga need to know?

Remember, Yoga is essentially a way of answering life's big questions – who am I? Why am I here? Where do I go after life? Or at least, it's a *way* of asking those questions. Furthermore, yoga consists of the various practices that help us experience a state of total presence.

From the perspective of history then, when did people start using Yoga to answer life's big questions, and when did they start using yoga practices to experience a state of total presence?

The short answer is a long, long, long time ago.

According to recent research by yogic scholar Georg Feuerstein, longer than we initially thought.

Thanks to satellite technology, recent mapping of areas of India shows that an ancient river, Saraswati, once ran through Northern India. That river was the cradle of the Indus-Saraswati Civilisation – one of the oldest and most technologically advanced civilisations in the world. It existed from about 3300–1300 BCE. Clay tablets have been found from this civilisation showing people sitting in a manner that looks like a meditation posture. Add to that the existence of *The Vedas* – a collection of ancient spiritual texts – from the same time period, and 'voila!', that's when yoga must have started.

Of course, this yoga is nothing like the yoga we think we know today. They didn't practice postures in the way that we do at all. No, the introduction of asana and our intense focus on asana in the 21st century is a far more recent phenomenon in the world of yoga. But first, let's track Yoga through the texts we have from that time in Indian history.

After the four *Vedas*, dated from around 3300–1300 BCE,* we have *The Upanishads*, comprising at least 200 texts, some of which mention yoga frequently. These date from about 1000–500 BCE. One of these texts is *The Mahabharata*, an epic Sanskrit poem that includes a section called *The Bhagavad Gita*.

The Gita, as it's often called, is a 700-verse dialogue between Prince Arjuna and his chariot driver, who just happens to be Lord Krishna. Prince Arjuna is about to go into battle but can see friends and relatives on both sides of the battlefield, so wants to lay down arms. Who wants to kill their friends and relatives on the battlefield? Lord Krishna says: 'No, you can't do that, and here's why'.

The dialogue that ensues between Prince Arjuna and Lord Krishna discusses in depth the various means and ways to attain liberation, or enlightenment.

There are many ways to interpret the meanings of this great poem, all of which depend upon the perspective of the person doing the interpretation. It's often seen as an allegory for the ethical and moral difficulties of being a human being. *The Gita* was written sometime between 500 BCE and 200 BCE, and includes detailed

---

* Note: There is debate about these dates, as scholars disagree on when *The Vedas* were written.

references to three paths of Yoga – Karma, Bhakti and Jnana (see the next chapter for more on those).

It's notable that *The Gita* doesn't mention Raja Yoga, which includes Hatha Yoga – the physical path of yoga that we're all so familiar with. That falls to Patanjali in the next seminal yogic text, *The Yoga Sutras* – although the Raja Yoga that Patanjali expounds doesn't include any Hatha Yoga either. Hatha Yoga comes later, around 1500 CE.

Again scholars can't agree on when *The Yoga Sutras* were written – Feuerstein dates it as likely around 200 CE although says it could be as early as 200 BCE. Nor can they agree on Patanjali's role. Did he author the work himself or is it a collection drawing on other, earlier texts? It's one of those two things, or perhaps both of them. Maybe he drew heavily on earlier texts but also wrote some new material. Regardless, *The Yoga Sutras* are one of the foundational texts of yoga, where Patanjali lays out an eight-limbed approach to enlightenment that includes asana, pranayama and meditation (see the following chapter).

Patanjali's *Yoga Sutras* – whether written by him, compiled by him or edited by him – mark the first time yoga was codified into a system and written down.

This yoga and all the way up to about 1500 CE was mostly about transcending the body, attaining liberation and likely included no postures at all. However, Tantra practitioners were using practices that revolved around purifying the body as the temple.

What's Tantra? Not sex, if that's what you're thinking. Tantra is a philosophy or way of approaching life that has been around for thousands of years. It encompasses all things yogic. The word Tantra refers to a teaching, and there are hundreds of Tantric texts. Tantra adepts developed all kinds of practices for cleansing and clearing the body physically, mentally, emotionally and energetically.

3. Yoga Philosophy, History & Concepts

Tantra uses asana, pranayama, meditation, mantras, visualisation and some downright strange practices – at least to our minds.
Practices such as going into graveyards to find fresh corpses and
sitting in meditation on that corpse all night long. Why? To face
the reality that you will die, that everything dies, and that all is im-
permanent. What better way to viscerally come to this realisation
than by sitting on a corpse meditating? This is the core philosophy
of Tantra, that anything and everything can be used to liberate
oneself.

The development of Hatha Yoga, emerging out of Tantra, really
took off with the publication of *The Hatha Yoga Pradipika* in the
15th century CE. Written by Svatmarama, this text focuses on the
purification of the physical body leading to the purification of the
mind and prana (life-force). It's the first time we actually get textual
references to postures as we know them today. Now we *know* that
yogis are starting to use physical postures in their practice – which
is still firmly focused on liberation or self-realisation.

The modern history of yoga starts in the mid 19th century
when a Bengali physician and scientist called N. C. Paul published
Treatise on Yoga Philosophy. However, the first Hindu teacher to
bring yoga to the West and really get this party started was Swami
Vivekananda. He caught the attention of many Western philoso-
phers including Emerson, Hegel and Schlegel and notably spoke
at the Parliament of the World's Religions in 1893. Again, this
wasn't yoga as postures, this was yoga as a path to liberation. He
was sharing the yogic worldview, which was thoroughly rooted in
The Vedas, those Hindu texts from thousands of years ago. Swami
Vivekananda did teach breathing and meditation, but there was
little emphasis on physical postures. In fact, Mark Singelton suggests in his book *Yoga Body The Origins of Modern Posture Practice*
that Vivekananda shunned Hatha Yoga as because it was distaste-
ful or unsuitable.

In 1920, Paramahansa Yogananda travelled to the United States and set up the Self-Realisaton Fellowship, which still has its headquarters in Los Angeles. But Hatha Yoga as we know and love it possibly didn't enter America until 1947 when Indra Devi came back from her time in India. She studied with Krishnamacharya – the Godfather of Modern Yoga. He taught Iyengar (briefly), Pattabhi Jois, Indra Devi and T.K.V. Desikachar (his son). So where did he get his yoga from? It certainly wasn't from any of the ancient yoga texts, with the exception of *The Hatha Yoga Pradipika*.

Recent research by Mark Singleton also suggests that Krishnamacharya drew heavily on gymnastics traditions from Europe when he created his Vinyasa Flow sequences – particularly Ashtanga Vinyasa Yoga as taught by Pattabhi Jois. From the teachings of Krishnamacharya we have Iyengar Yoga, Ashtanga Yoga, Power Yoga, Vinyasa Yoga, Viniyoga and Yin Yoga.

This implies that the physical nature of yoga as we know it has roots in European gymnastics.

But there were other notable Indian teachers in the early 20th century, including Swami Sivinanda, Yogi Bhajan – who brought Kundalini Yoga to the West - and Swami Satyananda. These styles of yoga still used some postures, but also focused on pranayama, meditation and kriyas (purification practices, mantras and visualisation). There was none of the strong, physical practices coming from Krishnamacharya's lineage (it's worth noting here that Krishnamacharya was introduced to yoga at age 5 when his father began to teach him *The Yoga Sutras*. The father told the young boy that their family had descended from a revered ninth-century yogi, Nathamuni).

Gradually, in the 1970s, 1980s and finally the 1990s, Hatha Yoga postures were extracted from the more esoteric elements of yoga and presented to Westerners as purely physical endeavours – ways to increase flexibility and get fit.

But the real nature of yoga – as self-realisation – has never been lost. Krishnamacharya may have been drawing on European gymnastics when he put together some of his sequences but that yoga was still thoroughly rooted in an understanding of the flow of prana. The postures still work to create a state of yoga.

Today's modern yoga as taught by teachers like Donna Farhi, Shiva Rea, Mark Whitwell, Sarah Powers, Duncan Peak, Amy Ippoliti, Peter Sanson and Eion Finn may have strong physical components but all of those teachers are thoroughly grounded and rooted in the yogic tradition. They teach yoga in its fullest expression, using the postures as the entry point.

Modern yoga can still lead to self-realisation, although it's likely that a modern yoga practice needs to encompass more than asana if you are serious about self-realisation. Usually, once asana has freed and cleared the body, there is a natural movement toward pranayama and meditation. We're a long way from *The Vedas* yet nothing has been lost and everything stands to be gained.

Yoga texts: the Bhaga what?

Make no mistake – reading the ancient yoga texts can be tough going; yet ultimately it is rewarding. Some of these texts are thousands of years old and they are dense. A two-line sutra (thread) packs a serious punch. There are layers and layers of meaning behind the words, which take time to filter into one's consciousness.

Yet if you're just starting yoga, I wouldn't recommend reading any of the ancient texts – there's just no real need. Unless you're the literary type and enjoy studying ancient works it is easy to get put off and bogged down. It can read like a whole lot of mumbo jumbo. Not only do the texts describe obscure practices and states of consciousness, they can be downright weird at times.

However, once you've been practicing yoga for a while, you may find yourself curious and naturally drawn to read this text or that. In the reading, you may discover states of consciousness or experiences that you've been having. It's like recognition – there's a sense of 'a-ha!'. The texts cease to be so dense and strange and instead relate to what you've already experienced.

I didn't dive into any yoga texts until I did my yoga teacher training with Shiva Rea. She recommends a number of texts as part of the study, and I choose one called *The Song of the Sacred Tremor*. It's one of the Tantras, and I fell in love with the flow and the language. It also described aspects of my yoga practice, which I'd never read about anywhere else. It felt like coming home to something I already knew.

At their essence, that is what these texts are – simply the travelogues of other yogis who have traveled this way before. Imagine reading *A Rough Guide to Somalia* when you've never been anywhere outside of your hometown. Now imagine reading that same Rough Guide while you're travelling overland in Somalia. Suddenly the text becomes relevant and engaging and has so much more wisdom to offer you.

It's the same with the yogic texts. It's helpful to be traversing the same terrain before you dive in – and there is so much to dive into! I've already touched on some of the yogic texts in the previous chapter; so now let's take a more in-depth look at what they are.

The oldest recorded yoga philosophy shows up in *The Vedas*, which are a collection of sacred texts from India. Hindus consider *The Vedas* a direct transmission from God, so they are comparable to the Bible or the Quran. Yoga philosophy only gets a brief mention though and some might suggest we're reading too much into it.

The next major text to mention yoga is *The Upanishads* – again a collection of texts considered a direct transmission from God. These date from about 1000–500 BCE. Yoga gets more coverage this time but again it's mostly yoga philosophy on show. This is not yoga as physical postures, but yoga as consciousness.

The Mahabharata Upanishad is an epic mythical and historical account of the founding of India. I've already mentioned one section of this epic – *The Bhagavad Gita*, our next major yogic text.

The name *Bhagavad Gita* means *The Song of God* – in essence, God is singing the nature of life. 700 verses are divided into 18 chapters, in three sections. One section relates to Karma Yoga – the yoga of actions. Another refers to Bhakti Yoga, the yoga of devotion and the final section is Jnana Yoga, the yoga of knowledge. You'll recognise these as three of the four paths of Yoga.

Over the course of the text, Krishna explains the meaning of life, including the nature of the immortal Self (or Atman) and the correct way to reach Brahman (God). It is clear instructions for awakening – for peeling back the ego and seeing who we truly are. There is no mention of the path of yoga we know as Hatha Yoga, which is the entry point for most Westerners.

Finally, with the writing of *The Yoga Sutras* sometime between 200 BCE and 200 CE we have some practical instructions for yoga. Written by Patanjali – as far as we know, perhaps he was just the editor – there are 196 sutras or threads, divided into four sections. The eight limbs of yoga come from the second chapter of the sutras. This is the first time that asana has been mentioned in any of the yogic texts, and then in reference to a 'seat', as in, a comfortable way to sit in meditation.

About a thousand years later, a yogi called Svatmarama wrote *The Hatha Yoga Pradipika* (*Light on the Forceful Yoga*). It's still not yoga as we think we know it, but many fundamental concepts from Hatha Yoga are introduced and explained, such as kriya, bandhas, and mudras. Plus, for the first time, we have asanas as we know it introduced and explained.

Beyond these well-known texts, there are also likely hundreds more, particularly from Kashmir, in what is now Pakistan. This area was the birthplace of Kashmiri Shaivism, which developed between the eighth and twelfth centuries. These teachings, or Tantras, outline many practices of Tantra Yoga. And no, it's not all about sex, although sex was a part of some practices at times.

This era is where the Tantric text I already mentioned, *Yoga Spandakarika* or *Song of the Sacred Tremor,* arises from. It is suggested that this yoga is the form that preceded Hatha Yoga (remember *The Hatha Yoga Pradipika* was written in 1500 CE, at least 700 to 300 years after the flourishing of Shaivism).

Another of the ancient Tantras is *Vijnanabhairava,* or *Divine Consciousness.* In some ways, it's the most direct of all the yoga texts. In this text, yoga is used as both the awareness, or the transformation of human consciousness into divine consciousness, and the means by which one attains that transformation. It is the goal and the path to the goal – a state of consciousness which is free of all thought-constructs.

In the text, the Devi (or Goddess) asks, how can that state of divine consciousness be achieved? What follows is 112 answers – or 112 types of yoga. That is, 112 ways to transform human consciousness into divine consciousness. Some of these are even asana, but many are methods of concentration or meditation. For example, Verse 25 suggests that focusing the attention on the slight gap before the inhale turns into the exhale, and the exhale turns into the inhale, is one way to practice and attain yoga.

If you do any real study of the wide variety of yoga texts available – and not just the go-to texts of *The Yoga Sutras* and *The Bhagavad Gita* – it becomes clear that yoga is all about consciousness and attaining a particular state of being. Yes, asana is mentioned, as are various practices to attain these states of being, but there is never any question as to what "yoga" really is.

Even now, I can pick up one of the texts – usually *Song of the Sacred Tremor* – and just in reading a sutra or two I can feel a slight shift in consciousness. The text is a reminder of the larger context of life, and of yoga. It's a reminder that there have been thousands of people studying and immersing themselves in the transformation of consciousness for thousands of years.

Yet although one can learn much from reading these texts, there is no need to proclaim them as the ultimate authority on anything.

Just because they're old, and multi-layered, and often believed to be divine-inspired doesn't mean that you have to take them at face value or believe them or bow down to them. The very essence of Yoga is a questioning and inquiring nature. These texts reveal the internal experiences of yogis who lived in a particular time and place. Use them instead as a jumping off place, a way to question and explore your own experience. Ask questions of the text and see how it relates to your own experiences. In this way, the ancient writings become a form of teaching, and ultimately, that is the way to approach them.

What is this text about?

What can I learn from it?

How does it relate to my experience?

What can I take from it?

The four paths of yoga

The truth is one but the paths are many.

Swami Vishnu-devananda

By now, you'll have realised that yoga is about far more than just physical postures. Yoga is a wide variety of tools and practices that ultimately liberate us from identification with the ego or small Self. This liberation is also Yoga – a state of union where we perceive ourselves as part of All that Is.

These tools and practices of yoga, which led to Yoga, are generally categorised under four main paths. Three of these were introduced in *The Bhagavad Gita* – Jnana, Bhakti and Karma. The fourth path, Raja Yoga, was introduced by Patanjali in *The Yoga Sutras*. So these paths are thousands of years old.

Jnana Yoga

This path of yoga is most attractive to those with a philosophical or intellectual temperament – the main instrument is the mind. A Jnani Yogi studies the ancient texts directly – like Swami Satyananda. He immersed himself in the Tantra texts, studying and learning what he could and then applying it to the way he taught yoga in the 20th and 21st century. This is how the practice of Yoga Nidra was re-discovered. It was a Tantra practice that Swami Satyananda found in the texts and modified for modern people.

On this path, the seeker uses his will and the power of discrimination to cut through the veil of ignorance and attain the truth – the truth being self-realisation or liberation. Jnana is about wisdom, knowledge, introspection and contemplation, with the goal being absolute truth.

An example of a practice of the Jnani is studying the scriptures of Yoga, or studying the workings of his own psyche. Through these practices, one comes to know oneself – and what is not actually oneself.

Bhakti Yoga

Those with a more emotional temperament who feel things deeply may be more attracted to the path of Bhakti. This is the devotional path of love toward God or Source. This kind of love is called Prem – it's pure, unconditional, divine love. A Bhakti uses all their emotions and transmutes them into Prem, and that Prem is directed to Source, or God, creating a direct relationship with the divine.

An example of a Bhakti Practice is Kirtan, or devotional chanting. Most chanting is done in Sanskrit and often contains mostly the various names of the Gods – which one can see as aspects of the Self. Through chanting, over and over and over and over again, these Sanskrit words create a shift in consciousness (see the chapter *'What are you OM about?'*). There are nine Bhakti practices in total, and all aim to maintain direct contact with God – which is what makes Kirtan a Bhakti practice.

This is a subtle, but powerful energetic practice that is accessible to anyone.

Raja Yoga

This path appeals to those with a mystical and scientific temperament. Think Einstein! Yes, Yoga recognises that the scientist and the mystic are the same, each seeking a true experience of reality. This is the path of self-control and mastery, achieved through perfect mind control, which can be accessed through the use of the body – i.e. via postures.

The main practice in Raja Yoga is meditation – remember Patanjali, who described Yoga as the cessations of the fluctuations of the mind and was the first to introduce this path of yoga in writing. This path is where Hatha Yoga arises; Hatha Yoga is the physical yoga that we in the West know and love. The purpose of Hatha Yoga is to balance the body and mind, bringing opposites together (masculine/feminine, soft/hard, sun/moon, active/passive, hot/cold).

Karma Yoga

This path appeals to those of us with an active temperament – think Richard Branson. Yes, business people have a path of yoga too! This is the path of pure action – seeing what needs to be done and doing it with no thought of one's own attainment or results. Karma Yogis challenge the notion that we're all inherently selfish by opening their hearts through selfless service and seeing God in all beings. The energy behind any action is the key aspect in Karma Yoga – if there is any kind of emotional motivation or ulterior motive behind an action, it is considered impure.

If you go and spend time in an Ashram, you are likely to be instructed in Karma Yoga. I have a dear friend and yogi who studied with Swami Satyananda and he tells tales of being asked to scrub the toilets, and all the feelings and thoughts this brought up in him. Yet he still had to do it, over and over again, working with those thoughts and feelings until they dissolved and he was able to clean the toilets simply as pure action, with no emotional motivation or ulterior motive in doing so.

However, you don't have to go to an Ashram to experience Karma Yoga – in many ways it's one of the most accessible paths of yoga available to us. We all have work to do, whether paid or unpaid. Karma Yoga asks us to bring total awareness to how we do that work and what it brings up in us when we do. It asks us to let go of anything impure that might be motivating us, so we cease to take action in the world for gain or results, and instead take action because that action is the right action for our path.

These four paths all work together, and most of us will find a blend of the four paths that suits our lifestyle and temperament best. We may be practicing Hatha Yoga, working to still our minds through Raja Yoga, while also learning to take action with a pure heart. We may study the ancient scriptures so as to better understand the depths of Yoga while also having a strong physical practice. We may go to Kirtan weekly and have a daily mediation practice.

It's important to understand that these definitions and classifications separate out Yoga in a way that is only to serve as a concept. Don't get too hung up on knowing the paths, or knowing which practice belongs to which path. It's not necessary, all you need to know is that Yoga is more than the postures. You may be attracted to yoga and not want to do any postures and that's okay – there is likely a practice that suits you perfectly.

For most of us, when we first start yoga – 'I'm going to yoga classes' – it would be more accurate to say that we're attending posture classes, or asana class. This is only one sliver of the world of yoga. Over time, we begin to realise that yoga is a full-spectrum experience that affects our body, mind, emotions and life.

Ultimately, yoga is calling our attention to what is real and what is unreal. Through our practice of physical postures, we begin to break down and change our bodies, and therefore, often our patterns of behaviour. Where once we had tight hamstrings and felt like we had to keep a strong grip or control over life, we find that our hamstrings have loosened and so too has our grip on life. An aspect of Self that we always thought was part of who we were – *'Oh, I'm a control freak.'* – changes. It is us no longer. The real has been revealed to be unreal.

In this way, yoga is a process of destruction and clearing away of our ego structures. Through purifying the body and mind, and developing our ability to concentrate we discover a new ground of being – that which is the real.

Initially, this all sounds nice in theory, but scarcely real or relevant. We're so identified with our personalities and our ego structures that we scarcely know they exist – it's just who we are.

'I am a control freak', you say. Yet you are not. You experience a pattern of controlling. Once you develop the Witness through the practice of yoga postures, you can see that pattern of control when it arises, and you can choose to engage with it or not. You can change the pattern.

How you change patterns, the practices you immerse yourself in – these are the four paths. Find the practice and the path that suits you and you will feel at home – whether its Raja Yoga with its postures and meditation, Karma Yoga with its pure action, Bhakti Yoga with its loving devotion to All that Is or Jnana Yoga with its study of scriptures and the self.

In the end, it's all the same.

You realise your Self.

The eight limbs of yoga

As you found out in the chapter on Yogic Texts, one of the most famous yogic texts is *The Yoga Sutras*. These were either written by, or compiled and edited by a man named Patanjali. He was the first person to codify Yoga in a system – or at least, to do so in a written form.

Over the course of 196 sutras or threads, Patanjali expounds on exactly what Yoga is and how to attain it or practice it. His method refers to 'eight limbs' – as in limbs on a tree. These limbs are not necessarily concurrent – you don't attain limb #1 before moving on to Limb #2. No, each limb develops alongside the others, sometimes concurrently.

Much is made of the fact that in these 196 sutras Patanjali only mentions the word 'asana' three times, and then in its context as seat, rather than necessarily posture. This is the major difference between Yoga as we perceive it now, and Yoga as it is. One of the *tools* of practicing and attaining yoga – asana – has become synonymous with Yoga itself. Very often, we confuse the posture for the yoga.

When you read through Patanajali's *Yoga Sutras*, this becomes clear. The 196 sutras are organised into four chapters, called Pada (which also means feet/foot, further extending the idea of eight limbs). These Pada or chapters are called *Concentration, Practice, Progression* and *Liberation*. There's a clear movement from one state of being to another and through to self-realisation. Just to make it clear, Patanajali starts by telling us *exactly* what Yoga is – the cessations of the fluctuations of the mind, or mastery of the activities of the mind.

In chapter 2, *Practice*, Patanjali states that discrimination is the key for enlightenment and that there are eight rungs or limbs – tools if you will – that lead to discrimination. These eight limbs – literally Ashtanga in Sanskrit, are laid out as follows.

The first two are Yamas and Niyamas.

Yamas are our own personal ethics or how we behave in the world. There are five of them:

- Ahimsa: Non-violence
- Satya: Truthfulness
- Asteya: Non-stealing
- Brahmacharya: Being in integrity with your sexual energy
- Aparigraha: Non-covetousness

Niyamas are how we behave toward our self – self-discipline.

Again, there are five of them.

- Saucha: Cleanliness
- Santosa (or Samtosha): Contentment
- Tapas: Heat; Spiritual austerities
- Svadhyaya: Study of the sacred scriptures and of one's self
- Isvara Pranidhana: Surrender to God

These are not so much moral guidelines or ten commandments but behaviours that naturally begin to arise through one's yoga practice. For example, practicing asana is automatically an act of Svadhyaya or self-study.

You are observing yourself in postures, listening to your breath, watching your mind, tuning into the sensations of the body, and learning to stay with whatever arises. This staying with whatever arises is Isvara Pranidhana, or surrender to God. If the word God makes you squirm, think of it instead as surrendering to the moment. It's fully accepting what is, as it is, right now.

Our practice also teaches us non-violence, in the way we treat our body and approach asana. It teaches Satya – we learn to be truthful about what we're experiencing, allowing emotion to arise, acknowledging that we need to modify this posture, or back out right now, or push ourselves further past our edge.

Over time, as you immerse yourself in yoga, it becomes clear how following the Yamas and Niyamas reduces your suffering in daily life. It's like lightening the load and cutting the strings. These guidelines aren't so much moral directives or commandments, but the natural unfolding tendencies of a yogi in process.

The third limb Patanjali mentions is asana. Now this word means posture, but it also means 'seat', as in mediation seat – the way one sits for meditation. It's entirely possible that it's *only* in this context that Patanajli was using it. That one learns to find a comfortable seat. This is crucial in yoga practice, because without the ability to sit comfortably for long periods of time it is impossible to do pranayama or meditation. These are the fourth and fifth limbs of Ashtanga Yoga.

Asana practice also purifies our body – physically, mentally, emotionally and energetically. It makes us healthier, stronger and strengthens our nervous system. This process increases our sensitivity to our internal processes – whether they are mental, emotional, physical or energetic. That's why Krishnamacharya was able to stop his heart beating at will, or slow down his breath cycle on demand.

Through asana practice, we become far more connected to our bodies and minds, and more comfortable within our bodies.

As already mentioned, the fourth limb in *The Yoga Sutras* is pranayama. While this word is usually translated as breathing practices, it really refers to one's ability to work with prana, or life-force. Generally, this is done through breathing exercises because the breath and prana are intimately linked.

The fifth, sixth and seventh limb are all aspects of concentration or meditation. Pratyahara is the drawing of one's attention away from things – such as sounds, smells, sights, tastes or feeling sensations. Instead, one withdraws from the senses into the internal space.

Pratyahara teaches us to focus our attention solely on the internal space – which means our thoughts. Dharana now takes that attention on our thoughts and teaches us how to focus it completely – that means our thoughts begin to slow down and perhaps one day even stop. Or at least, pause for a few minutes at a time.

The final step in this honing of our awareness – first withdrawing into the internal space then focusing on a single point in that space – is Dhyana, when we learn to sustain that awareness no matter what. This is the uninterrupted flow of concentration. No thought can cause us to waver.

Whereas in Dharana we often use a single point of focus – perhaps our breath, or gazing at a candle, in Dhyana there is nothing but awareness itself. The need to focus that awareness has dissipated and we are simply aware.

Out of this arises the final limb, Samadhi, or Bliss. This is the point of union where our perception of ourselves merges back into the great consciousness. It's like we are a drop of water becoming the ocean again. The subject observing the object becomes one and the same.

Looking at these eight limbs, it's clear that the main focus is our attention – where we place it and how we expand it. Everything else serves that purpose. Asana is a tool to teach us awareness and focus, as is pranayama.

When you first start to attend yoga classes, you don't need to know anything about *The Yoga Sutras*, or the eight limbs. As you progress, you may begin to have questions and at some point, you may want to get yourself a copy of *The Yoga Sutras* and read it for yourself.

Like most of the yogic texts, reading something like *The Yoga Sutras* takes time and concentration. It's only short – 196 lines, very few words – but the depth of those words is endless. If you study *The Sutras* with a teacher, often you'll take one couplet and study that for a week, before moving on to the next.

It's easy to revere and bow down before a text like *The Yoga Sutras*, honoring it as supreme wisdom. Yet it is only one of the many texts that talk about Yoga. It's not that the text might be wrong, but there are other ways you may look at the same concepts – received wisdom is not always ultimate truth, it's just a pit-stop along the way.

Matthew Remski is the author of *Threads of Yoga* which is a remix of *The Yoga Sutras*. He's used numerous translations and commentaries to piece together a version of *The Yoga Sutras* that distills down the essence of Yoga and consciousness within a modern and post-modern context.

If I was picking up a translation of *The Yoga Sutras* for the first time, I'd be tempted to buy *Threads of Yoga,* as Matthew speaks in a language that is accessible and meaningful to our modern lives, while also adding his own philosophy and comments. This helps to keep the Yoga alive – showing that it's not something that was created or discovered thousands of years ago and is now held in stone, but something that is forever evolving and changing as we evolve and change.

Yet within this evolution and change, *The Sutras* remain timeless – able to stand and grace us with as much wisdom as they did two thousand years ago. It's entirely possible that Remski's modern interpretation and remix will also stand for two thousand years and in millennium from now, students of Yoga will learn about Remski as they do Patanjali.

After all, we have Patanjali's texts, but we don't know of the man himself. Nor do we know of other great texts that might have been lost to the passages of time.

Yes, *The Sutras* offer wisdom and they point the way. But they are not the way.

Intro to Kleshas & Gunas

Practicing asana gives us the opportunity to observe our relationship with the postures, with our bodies, with our minds and with our breath. This relationship is what reveals ourselves to ourselves. Asana is a powerful tool to access our psyches, release tension in the body and help us understand the hidden aspects of Self.

In other words, paying attention to questions like this is how we use asana to awaken.

- Are you liking the pose?
- Are you disliking the pose?
- Or are you completely absent from the pose as you think about what you're going to have for dinner tomorrow night?

Being aware of your thoughts and *where* your attention is going takes your asana practice to the next level – it takes it into Yoga. This awareness opens up yoga philosophy on the mat – and yoga philosophy (simply the study of the psyche) directly answers *everything* that is going to come up on your mat. It answers your fears, your anxieties, your tension, your discomfort, your emotions and your thoughts.

There is so much to learn about yoga philosophy you can spend a whole lifetime studying it – and lots of yogis have done just that. They've studied the fluctuations of the mind, the psyche, the body – and they know how all of these things work together.

But these yogis weren't reading books to gain these understandings, they were reading their body and mind on the mat (and off) and then passing on everything they experienced for later yogis like you and I to read all about – and then discover for ourselves on the yoga mat.

For example, there are the Kleshas, described as obstacles of the mind and five in total. These obstacles of mind block you from truth.

- Avidya: Ignorance – thinking something is true when it's not – like yoga is just for women. Uh-uh!
- Asmita: Egosim – identifying with the mind, thinking that *you* are your thoughts. Not true!
- Raga: Attachment – having to have something. Like a certain spot for your mat in class every week or it ruins your class. Only because you *think* it will!
- Dvesa: Aversion – avoiding something. Like handstand because you're afraid of it.
- Abhinivesah: Fear of death – okay, pretty big, and the entire crux of getting to enlightenment. Fear of death often arises in class as fear of letting go and surrendering into the practice.

Practicing asana begins to reveal the way our mind works and the obstacles it throws up – the Kleshas.

When you're on your mat and the teacher says, 'Now we're going to do Crow Pose' and your mind thinks 'Oh I hate crow' – that's aversion. And aversion leads to suffering, which is what we're working to release when we practice yoga. If you're new to practice and new to asana, you're likely to let that thought determine your experience. You won't wholeheartedly listen to the instructions or allow yourself to surrender into the posture.

However, as you become more experienced in the practice, you'll recognise this thought as an obstacle to practice, you'll let it go, come back to your breath, and go into Crow with a beginner's mind as if you've never done it before so you don't know what it's like. Because it's not *like* anything. It's just Crow.

Over time, as you do the same postures in class after class after class after class, you'll observe that your experience of those postures shifts and changes – and you'll notice that your experience of those postures is dependent upon your thoughts and feelings about those postures.

This is a huge lesson to learn, and a big step toward self-realisation. It comes through a combination of asana practice and awareness of your relationship *to* asana practice.

Case in point.

For years, when I practiced Bikram Yoga, I would get to Standing Bow pose and I would start to cry. Something about going into that posture just broke me open and I would end up with tears streaming down my face for the rest of class.

Over time, I started to fear coming into Standing Bow Pose, fear for the tears that were going to arise, fear for the experience I was going to have. I would notice myself thinking as we approached the posture 'I hate Standing Bow Pose' – I would literally stiffen up before we even began the set-up for Standing Bow.

Finally, I noticed myself doing this and I wondered – 'What would happen if I changed my thoughts? Would my experience of the posture change?'

The next time we approached Standing Bow Pose, I told myself, 'I love this pose, I love this pose, I love this pose'. I was totally faking it, but it shifted something in my body and my physical experience of the posture was difference – there was more ease and more softness.

That was a watershed moment for me – understanding that the *way* I approached the postures and what I thought and felt about them completely influenced my experience of them.

Even though I'd been doing Standing Bow Pose all those classes, I'd been subtly avoiding it – holding against it – and this is one of the obstacles of the mind, aversion.

You don't need to study the Kleshas or know them inside out to gain more benefit out of your asana practice. You *do* need to bring awareness to what you think and feel in relation to your practice.

When you see or feel the same thing coming up repeatedly – if you notice that you get angry if someone else takes your favourite spot in the room – then it shows there's something to work with.

Then it can be useful to go away and do some yogic reading. Read up about the Kleshas at that point and see if deepening your understanding of these concepts helps you to understand yourself and your practice better.

However, it's not just the Kleshas which describe what we might experience in relation to our yoga practice, there's also the Gunas, or states of mind, three in total. The Gunas describe the general feeling of your thoughts.

- Sattva – balance, order, purity. This is how you maybe feel after class. Everything is just cool. You feel calm and centred and blissed out. This is contentment.

- Rajas – energetic, active, frantic. This is when you feel motivated and all fired up to do something, but it can also be too frantic.

- Tamas – lethargic, dull, slow. This is how you feel when you're depressed and can't be bothered. It's when you're glued to your couch or just can't get yourself out the door to practice.

When we practice yoga, we learn that no matter *what* our state of mind before class – generally Rajas or Tamas – simply by turning up and getting on our mat, we can shift that state of mind towards Sattva.

We learn not to wallow in Tamas;

'Oh I can't be bothered, don't feel like it.'

Or not to storm about in Rajas, totally pumped and charging from one thing into the next.

Instead of accepting that state of mind as just the way we are, we recognise that we are ultimately masters of our minds and we can take action to shift our state – like doing some asana practice or chanting or doing pranayama.

We also learn that's it also okay to just accept our state of mind for what it is right now, and not let it throw us off course. Even though we feel lethargic and slow, we still turn up and do what we have to do.

Through constant observation of our mind and the states of being that it fluctuates through we begin to realise that our state of mind colours our experience.

Being aware of this means we can learn to see through that filter. We understand that because we feel lethargic and slow, everything *seems* dull and lifeless yet it's not. It is *we* who are dull and lifeless. In that recognition and acceptance of our state of being and state of mind, we have a choice – stay with it or take action to shift it. It doesn't matter which choice we make, either one means we are coming into our power.

Understanding just these two concepts of yogic philosophy – the Kleshas and the Gunas – can have a profound effect on your experience in yoga class.

It's all too easy to go to class and think you're doing yoga while getting all caught up in the web of liking/disliking/attachment/egosim/ignorance. Sure, your asana might be looking better and better... but your relationship to that asana hasn't shifted since the very first class.

In fact, it's possible for asana to become an obstacle to truth as your ego feeds on your yoga practice and it becomes just another thing you do that builds up your ego identity.

It's awareness that breaks this cycle and moves you beyond practicing physical postures and into practicing yoga, where the postures serve to illuminate your thoughts and feelings.

Knowing that yoga explains what's going on in the psyche in these easily digestible concepts helps us to understand what's happening on the mat, and what's happening in our relationship with our practice.

We begin to grasp what yoga really is and what it can do for us in our lives. It's total awareness of our moment-to-moment experience, and learning to meet that moment fully, as it is.

A quick tour through the Koshas

Do enough research, and it seems we can find evidence that regular practice of yoga positively impacts everything from anxiety, depression and panic attacks to thyroid conditions, sciatica and asthma.

In fact, it could be said that yoga can positively impact anything that has to do with the functioning of our physical bodies, minds or emotions.

How can this be possible?

Well no, it's not exactly. But it might be.

Yoga works to harmonise the body, mind and emotions by removing blockages on all levels of our system. The removal of these blockages allows our bodies, minds and emotions to function at their optimum level.

Remember, yoga is often referred to as the Science of Life – and with good reason.

Over the centuries, yogis have used the practice of yoga to experientially collect information about the way we function.

This information has been codified for easy explanation, and now the work of Western scientists is corroborating more and more of what the yogis learned experientially.

The yogis defined our body as having five layers or sheaths, each one contained within the other, like russian dolls.

Called Koshas, these sheaths cover every aspect of our being, from the most physical (gross being the correct term) to the most subtle. When we practice yoga – whether it's asana, pranayama, meditation, mantra or even Karma Yoga – we are having an impact on one or more of these layers of the body.

For example, asana will primarily affect the grossest layer of Kosha, Annamayakosha. Of course, anything that affects one Kosha will also affect the other Koshas because there is no real separation between the layers. They are a conceptual method of understanding that allows us to make sense of our experience.

When you understand that the practice of yoga works to release blockages in the many layers of the body it helps you understand why sometimes we resist – strongly resist – our practice.

Those blockages often hide fears and unexpressed emotions. Sure, yoga will make you feel great, but it will also make you feel.

Sometimes what we feel during or after yoga isn't wonderful, and it helps to have a conceptual model to understand why this can be.

Back to the Koshas, and I'll keep it short.

Kosha #1 is Annamayakosha – the outside layer of the body, and roughly translates as the food body

This is our physical body – our muscles and our bones, our ligaments and our tendons. This is the Kosha most people are concerned about when they begin a yoga practice. They want increased flexibility, they want to tone up their muscles, they want to learn to relax their bodies, and they're looking to gain strength, improve their balance and find stress relief.

The primary way to impact this Kosha is through asana.

The practice of asana will also impact Kosha #2, Pranamayakosha – the energy body

Like the Chinese have chi, the yogis have prana – or life force. Prana moves around the body via channels or Nadis. Some 72,000 apparently, although who counted them, nobody knows. When we practice asana and pranayama, we are impacting Pranamayakosha.

Any blockages in those nadis (and believe me, you'll have blockages) are worked through, bit by bit. Your improved flow of energy in the body can then affect the Annamayakosha and also impact any health issues you may be having.

Prana comes into the body via food and water, but it also comes into the body via breath. One of the major benefits of yoga is that we become conscious of our breathing, and – sometimes for the first time as adults – we learn to take proper deep breaths.

This increase of prana into our system literally makes us feel more alive and it invigorates and powers Pranamayakosha.

#3 on our tour of the Koshas is Manomayakosha, the mental body

People usually come to yoga for the physical benefits and *stay* because of how yoga impacts Manomayakosha. Put bluntly, you feel bloody great after class – mentally clear and emotionally upbeat. That's what keeps you coming back, time after time.

Manomayakosha is that aspect of Self which takes care of our instinctual needs, plus it also helps us obtain our individual desires. On a practical level that means it's about safety, security, obtaining love and taking care of loved ones.

If you're experiencing underlying anxiety because you've lost your job and you don't know how you're going to pay rent, you're experiencing that in Manomayakosha. A calming yoga practice like Alternate Nostril Breathing can alleviate those feelings and thoughts.

Most of us have a tendency to 'live' in one Kosha more than the others. Some people are body-orientated, in general Westerners tend to be mind-orientated. However, the practice of yoga helps us to balance out our awareness of *all* the layers of Self and shift us out of being primarily just in Manomayakosha.

This can mean that our anxiety fades somewhat. It will still be there, but we may be more grounded in Annamayakosha or Kosha #4 – Vijnanamayakosha, the wisdom body.

That grounding in the Wisdom body gives us a broader perspective on our life experience and we're able to see that we'll get another job, or that we have plenty of resources to call on. The anxiety fades.

Cultivating Kosha # 4 – Vijnanamayakosha is an unexpected benefit of yoga for most people

You turn up expecting an exercise class and wanting to touch your toes. But you find yourself connecting to a deeper level of intuition, greater internal wisdom and a sense of higher knowledge.

Deepening into an awareness of Vijnanamayakosha may take more than a class once a week, but if you continue to practice, it will come.

It's at this more subtle level of our Self that we begin to shift from a primary *I-ness* orientation – I am a separate being – to a primary *One-ness* orientation. We feel and understand, on a deep level that there is no real difference or separation from *me* and *you*.

We move beyond feelings and concern based on survival and security, and into feelings that encompass and include all – like compassion, love, and joy. Our relationships change, and become more fulfilling, and more joyous. Life simply becomes good. We're well along the path of yoga and that journey from ego/mind or small self to Soul or Big Self.

Shifting into Vijnanamayakosha is mostly about doing the work that removes the blockages in the three lower Koshas. We find comfort and harmony in our physical body, we release blockages in our energy body, and we heal and release fears from our mental body.

Finally, there's Kosha #5. Anandamayakosha, or the Bliss Body

Exactly as it sounds, it's all about the bliss baby. No longer separate, you're bathing in One-ness with All that Is. You and God, you're One and the Same. That's about all I'm going to say about Kosha #5, because if you're getting there, you don't need me to tell you about it; and if you're not there, I can't tell you about it, because I'm not there either. *Yet.*

As you practice, no matter what style or kind of yoga you're practicing, you're releasing blockages in one or more of these layers of the body. That can mean old memories – good or bad – floating to the surface of your consciousness. It can mean the spontaneous release of emotion like tears or laughter. It can mean jerking of the body as energy releases in strange ways.

All of this is normal.

All of this can be part of your yoga experience.

Kundalini, prana, nadis, chakras & the subtle body

Oh where to start, where to start! Entire books have been written about Kundalini, prana, Shakti, nadis, chakras and the subtle body – big fat books that double as steps for short people. Now I need to succinctly inform you of the basics in 1,000 - 2,000 words. Let's start with some definitions and go from there.

The subtle body contains all of these concepts we're going to talk about. As the name suggests, this body is not physically manifest – it's not like the fluid body, made up of synovial fluids or our circulatory system. No, the subtle body is purely energetic.

You can't sense it through the five senses – you can't touch it, smell it, see it, taste it or hear it. However, it is as real as the chair I'm sitting on as I write these words. How do I know? I can sense it... although I can't tell you how I'm sensing it.

But when I work with students, it's the subtle body I'm perceiving – where it's blocked, where it's flowing, where it's weak. Don't take my word for it though. The subtle body is not something I'm asking you to believe in. It's something that you will experience for yourself as you practice yoga and hone your ability to tune into what's going on in your body.

When we practice yoga, what we're really doing is affecting the subtle body, and as a result of that, our physical experience of reality shifts. This concept is not restricted to yoga though – many traditions reference the subtle body and its energy, including traditional Chinese medicine, Taoism, Tibetan Buddhism, and Shingon (which is Japanese).

There are two main aspects to the subtle body – the channels that the energy flows along, and the energy that flows along the channels. The channels are the same in everyone. It's like a system of canals that criss-cross the human body, and where there are major junctions of canals joining, imagine a circular pool like a roundabout where all the energy enters, circles and exits. Those major junctions are chakras. We'll come back to those, but first, the canals and the energy that travels along the canals.

The word used to describe the canal system is nadis, and traditionally there are 72,000 of them in the human body. That I can't verify, but there are some I can feel in my body and identify. The word 'nadi' means tube, or pipe. Instead of canals and water, you could also see it as the body's electrical system – nadis are wires that carry energy.

The three major nadis are Ida and Pingala, which start at the base of the spine and criss-cross up through the seven chakras to exit through the crown of the head. Ida is feminine, passive, lunar and Pingala is masculine, active, solar. When these two nadis flow evenly and strong, they help to clear and awaken the third major nadi, Sushumna. This is the central spine nadi and the most important wire in the body. Sushumna runs from the base of the spine all the way up to the crown of the head.

You may come across these terms in your yoga classes, and it is useful to understand what they refer to so you don't feel completely lost.

For example, Nadi Shoden Pranayama, or Alternate Nostril Breathing is a pranayama that aims to balance the left and right sides of the body and brain. On a subtle level, it's working directly with Ida and Pingala. On a body level, it helps us switch nervous systems – from the sympathetic nervous system (fight, flight or freeze) to the parasympathetic nervous system (rest and digest).

Often we can find ourselves out of balance – either feeling lethargic and slow or hyperactive and antsy. A pranayama like Alternate Nostril Breathing can energise us or calm us down, depending on where our deficiency is, and bring us back in a state of balance. If you understand that Ida is related to the left nostril and you notice that you are agitated and hyperactive, plus your left nostril is totally blocked and you're only breathing through the right nostril... you can do an experiment and see if Alternate Nostril Breathing helps the left nostril to open and calms you down.

Remember, yogis are scientists and their laboratory is their own body. Every time you practice, you bring full awareness and attention to your internal experience – the Inner-Verse. In this way, you begin to learn more and more about what's going on inside of you. Not just physically, but also emotionally, mentally, spiritually and energetically. In time, you begin to sense how these aspects of being are all linked.

If nadis are wires, the energy that travels along those wires is prana, or life force. Prana enters the body mostly through the breath, and it is intimately connected with the breath, but it is not the breath.

Most people when they start yoga have a shallow breath and the simple act of breathing properly through an entire class and bringing more prana into the body is one reason why you feel so great after a yoga class.

In time, as your awareness of the subtle body increases, you learn how to use your breath to direct prana around the body. You can literally breathe prana through the soles of your feet and into the earth, or through your hands and up into the sky.

Pranayama, which is often translated as breathing exercises, is far more than that. Yes, you're using the breath at all times, but because prana is carried within the breath, it's actually the life-force that you're working with. You could translate pranayama as life-force manipulation... as in Alternate Nostril Breathing when you use a breath exercise to ensure that prana is flowing evenly through two of the most important nadis – Ida and Pingala.

If prana is electricity, then Kundalini is the power station. In most people, this power station is old, disused and run down. There's only one old generator still pumping away. Because the power station has been running on 5% for so long, our wiring system has also fallen into disrepair and can no longer handle the high voltage power our power station is capable of delivering.

When we practice yoga, and particularly asana, we're strengthening our nadis – we're literally rewiring our bodies and getting ready to bring the power station back on line. More prana comes in through our breath and our wiring gets used to handling more charge.

In some people, as a result of yoga practice (although not always), the power station wakes up again. All the old generators power up and come back on line and huge amounts of energy surge out into the wiring system. If the correct yoga practices haven't been done, this surge of energy can blow wires and short-circuit the entire system, which can leave us physically, emotionally and mentally ill. This is known as Kundalini Syndrome. Our Kundalini has awakened, but we weren't ready to handle the energy.

Kundalini is an aspect of Shakti, which is the divine feminine energy out of which all energy arises.

As Kundalini is Shakti, so too is prana. Initially, we start with a smaller energy – prana, which leads us to a large energy, Kundalini, which awakens the biggest energy of all Shakti. When Kundalini awakens it begins to journey up the spine through Sushumna, heading for the crown of the head.

Most people have all kinds of blocks in their energy system so Kundalini doesn't get very far before hitting a block, or blowing some wiring and manifesting all kinds of physical, mental and emotional issues. Then we do the work required to clear that block, the issue dissipates and Kundalini Shakti is on the rise again; until the next block.

This process is yoga. Eventually, Shakti – the divine feminine energy – will rise unobstructed all the way to the crown of the head where she meets Shiva – the divine male consciousness. The re-union of Shakti and Shiva is the culmination of Yoga. It's union of energy and consciousness as the perceived separate Self dissolves in the ocean of All that Is.

And you thought you'd be able to stretch out your hamstrings, lose some weight, and build a bit of strength!

Me, I dig this stuff because it makes sense to me and I've had real world experiences that make it totally experiential for me. But until you feel your heart chakra opening, you don't have to worry about whether such a thing exists or not. It really doesn't matter.

All that you need to know – and maybe not even this – is that the subtle body is a map of the terrain that your psyche will travel during your yoga practice. Chakras are landscapes along the way that can help you make sense of your experience, if you need to do so. I'm not even going to list out the main seven chakras and what they're all about, because it doesn't matter. If your interest is tweaked and you want to know more, there are plenty of excellent books out there like Anodea Judith's *Western Body Eastern Mind*.

And if you are having energetic experiences in your yoga practice already, go find a copy of Stephen Cope's *Yoga and the Quest for the True Self*. It's an excellent guide that highlights just how normal all of this weird and wacky energetic stuff is.

Otherwise, you can just let it all go and get on to more real world concerns like what you might actually be doing in class, besides balancing out Ida and Pingala nadis.

4. YOUR YOGA PRACTICE

The practice: what can it include?

When we're new to yoga, our idea of what a yoga practice is conjures up images of beautiful bodies bending effortlessly into graceful shapes. Many of us think – 'that's not for me, I can't do that' – for reasons ranging from being too inflexible, too old, or too physically limited. As we looked at in an earlier chapter, *Common misconceptions about yoga*', none of those reasons are necessarily true.

We can practice yoga asanas (postures) despite being inflexible, despite being old(er) and despite our physical limitations. However, yoga is about so much more than just postures. You may have started to get an inkling of its breadth and depth in the chapter on '*Yoga philosophy, history and concepts*'.

Some of that stuff can seem pretty out there though. Okay, so I get that Ahimsa is one of the Yamas and it means non-harming, but what's that got to do with my yoga practice?

Plenty, as it turns out. But hold that thought for a moment.

Remember the four paths of yoga? Raja, Jnana, Bhakti and Karma Yoga; and how physical postures are part of Hatha Yoga which is part of Raja Yoga? Well, what about those other paths – what about Jnana Yoga, Bhakti Yoga and Karma Yoga? How can they shape your yoga practice and why don't we know more about these kinds of yoga?

For one, Hatha Yoga is very easy to photograph – it's distinctive and iconic. Put someone into Camel Pose or Upward Bow or Dancer's Pose – all beautiful backbends – and I bet 90% of the population would point at those photos and say, "That's Yoga".

However, if you were to take a photo of someone sitting in Easy Cross-Legged Pose and chanting, as one does for a Bhakti Yoga practice, I bet only 10% of the population would point at the photo and say, 'Yoga'.

Take a photo of someone cleaning a toilet mindfully and with no attachment to result or acclaim... and I doubt anyone would look at that photo and say Karma Yoga. Besides which, who wants to clean toilets as a yoga practice?

That's one reason why our idea of yoga is so focused on asana – it's easy to photograph and looks desirable.

Remember though, at its core, Yoga is a way of being, it's a path to realisation and it is the *practice* we do on the path to realisation. That practice can include many things – including meditation. This is another distinction that's important to remember – Yoga and meditation are not two separate things. They are one and the same.

Meditation is another technique or tool, as asana is a technique or tool, and it comes in many variations. Some of these include focusing on a mantra (which also makes it a mantra practice), gazing at a candle (a practice called Trataka), counting the breath or techniques like Vipassana.

If I'm meditating – however I'm doing it – I'm also practicing yoga. And often, if I'm practicing a tool of yoga like asana or pranayama, I'm also meditating. Asana is often called meditation in movement.

Ultimately, meditation is the practice we're heading towards with Raja Yoga, which encompasses Hatha Yoga, of which Patanjali writes about in his eight limbs of yoga. Those eight limbs break down some of the practices.

Third on the list is asana, Fourth is pranayama or breath work, the fifth, sixth and seventh limbs all refer to meditation.

When you go to a yoga class in a studio, 99% of classes will include asana. Hopefully 99% will also include pranayama – even if it's just bringing more awareness to breathing deeply. 50% of classes may include some meditation at the end. You could say that Shavasana, or Dead Man's Pose, is lying down meditation.

At the end of most yoga classes (one would like to think all yoga classes – Shavasana is vital for our nervous system after we stir everything up during class) students are asked to lie flat on their backs, with their eyes closed. This is Shavasana. As you lie there, you allow yourself to settle into the position, becoming still. No twitching or adjusting or wriggling. Just total stillness. From this place of stillness, you watch the thoughts that are arising in your mind and allow them to go. That's it. Every time a thought arises, you see it and release it, thus coming back to internal stillness.

This combination of asana, pranayama and meditation is probably the most common exploration of yoga today. It's where most people start their yoga journey.

Other aspects of yoga that may show up in your class include mudras – generally shapes made with the hands and fingers. For example, holding your hands in prayer position is a mudra; or connecting one finger with the thumb and placing your wrists on your knees when you're sitting cross-legged.

Mudras create flows of energy in the body and each mudra has a specific energetic effect.

Another aspect of yoga that you may come across is bandhas – or locks. These are similar to mudras in that they also work energetically with the flow of prana; bandhas seal aspects of our body to create a flow of energy.

Hasta Bandha is the hand seal. It's the precise way that the hands connect to the ground in postures like Downward Dog or Crow. When done with full awareness, Hasta Bandha creates a strong foundation with ease of flow through the hands. Other common bandhas are more internal – for example Mula Bandha and Uddiyana Bandha.

You may often hear teachers refer to these bandhas in class without taking the time to explain what they are. That can be frustrating and annoying; if you have a teacher that does this, catch them after class and ask for instruction on what these bandhas actually are.

Mula Bandha or the root lock, catches and lifts the energy from the very base of the spine and pulls it upward. Engaging Mula Bandha is subtle – teachers often describe it as engaging the muscles around the perineum, which sits between the genitals and anus. Over time, the contraction of Mula Bandha becomes more and more subtle until it is purely an energetic lock. You bring full awareness to the very root of the spine and draw the energy up.

Uddiyana Bandha is easier to understand, because a teacher can actually demonstrate it. It's pulling the abdominal muscles in towards the spine and slightly up towards the lower ribs. Like catching your breath almost, only you can still breathe while you're engaging Uddiyana Bandha.

There are other bandhas, but these are the ones you are most likely to encounter in your first yoga classes.

So many strange words to get your head around – asana, pranayama, mudras, bandhas... it's all Sanskrit, the original language of Yoga. Sanskrit is also the language of Kirtan or chanting.

In an ordinary yoga class, you may come across some chanting to either start the class or finish the class. Of all aspects of yoga, this one can be the most off-putting and strange for new students. So much so that I've devoted an entire chapter to it – '*What are you Om about?*'

Let's jump back to that held thought from the beginning of this chapter – ahimsa or non-violence.

The Yamas are one of Patanajali's eight limbs of yoga. This is also something that you might encounter in a yoga class, or not. Some teachers will teach in an integrated manner, where they use themes to explore yoga philosophy during the practice of asana.

In a practical manner, this might mean a teacher dedicating a class to ahimsa (non-violence). As you go through that particular class, a skilled teacher will draw your attention to the ways in which we approach the postures physically – are we being gentle with ourselves and making sure we do no harm?

A skilled teacher will also draw our attention to our self-talk, the way we speak to ourselves in our mind during class. It's so easy to berate ourselves if we fall out of a posture, or can't effortlessly melt into it the way our neighbour does. That kind of negative self-talk isn't kind or helpful. By bringing our awareness to ahimsa and the way we speak to ourselves, a skilled teacher will help us along the path of embodying all eight limbs of yoga.

This gives you a clearer idea of what an asana class might contain – it's not just about the postures!

However, there's so much more than just asana when it comes to yoga.

If you've decided you like the sound of Jnana Yoga, reading and studying yogic texts could be your yoga practice. Teachers like Tantric scholar Christopher Tompkins coordindate online classes that explore the meaning of individual Tantric texts. His classes usually start with meditation, and then go on to study the texts, before ending with meditation or chanting. While there's not usually any asana going on, the feeling post-class is very similar to post-asana class. Christopher's classes can sometimes include exploration of long-forgotten Tantra yoga practices that involve meditation, visualisation, mudras, bandhas and chanting. Again, the only asana is sitting cross-legged, but there's plenty of yoga going on. These practices focus more on the subtle aspects of yoga, but can be just as – if not more – powerful than asana classes.

If you've always loved music or singing, or are the kind of person that likes to devote yourself to something; you may naturally feel drawn to Kirtan, one of the practices of Bhakti Yoga, see the chapter on '*The Four Paths of Yoga*'.

During the chanting people sit cross-legged, or as the energy builds, they may stand and sway to the music or even dance. It's a powerful practice of surrender and love. Afterwards, participants experience deep bliss – I know because I've been there! It's an extraordinarily powerful practice. Who knew that chanting could have such an effect?

Finally, there's Karma Yoga or the yoga of pure action. This is the practice of presence and mindfulness that is most often found in Ashrams – or at least, actively practiced in Ashrams! You might be washing dishes, cooking dinner, cleaning the toilets or writing a book, all with no thought of achievement or attainment or acclaim or reward. It doesn't matter what you're doing – any activity can have the energy of Karma Yoga brought into it.

My attitude and experience of housework completely transformed through Karma Yoga. Instead of chores being something to get through, something to get done or something to be acknowledged for having done... I learned to enjoy the act of cleaning the toilet simply for what it was in the moment. In doing so, the cleaning became a pure action, which is the goal of Karma Yoga. There was immense satisfaction in this.

Even if practicing postures doesn't grab you right now, but you're still curious about this thing called yoga, there are many ways in which you can practice yoga. However, the reality for most people is that you'll start practicing yoga by going to an asana class, or perhaps a meditation class. There can be great variation in classes, depending on the teacher and the style, see the chapter on '*Yoga Styles*'.

Right now though, all you need to do is realise that the practice of Yoga can include many things, some of which aren't asana at all.

Yoga off the mat: yoga, relationships & life

It's likely you haven't even stepped on to a yoga mat yet, but it's never too early to talk about yoga off the mat.

Yes, yoga *off* the mat. I'm not talking about aerial yoga or partner yoga or standup paddle board yoga... forms of yoga which don't always use a mat. I'm talking about how the practice of yoga informs our entire relationship to life.

We've already covered the eight limbs of yoga in the chapter on *Yoga Philosophy, History and Concepts*. It's very easy to read through those eight limbs and dismiss it as some ancient moral code, or a deeper part of yoga that only very experienced yoga students need to worry about.

While it's true that when you're first starting yoga, you're mostly concerned with limb #3 – asanas or postures – there's nothing stopping you from also bringing full awareness into the rest of your life.

It's nothing difficult or complicated. It's simply bringing the same level of awareness to all of your interactions with life and other people as you bring to your body and your breath on the yoga mat.

For example, recently I was in a difficult conversation with an ex-partner. While I was listening and speaking to him, I was also observing myself listening and speaking to him – just like I was on a yoga mat and observing myself breathing and moving into yoga postures. In the same way that we're curious about what we experience on a yoga mat – 'what is that sensation in my hip, am I holding on to tension in my shoulders?' – I was being curious about how I was in this conversation.

I noticed that I was being extraordinarily passive. I felt like I had nothing to say. I inquired into that and realised that I didn't want to upset or hurt him. Yet my concern for his feelings was silencing my voice. My present moment awareness during this difficult conversation meant I was able to see myself as if from the outside and consciously choose to respond in a different way. I was able to *choose* to speak up, with compassion. When I did so, I felt the energy of our exchange shift and my energy shift. Instead of avoiding the situation, I was accepting it and working with it.

This is yoga off the mat and this is where yoga really gets interesting. It's nothing fancy or complicated. It's awareness of what we're thinking and feeling as we're thinking and feeling it.

Instead of being so mired in our experience that we identify with our thoughts and feelings, we've learned to shift our state of being back to *awareness* of those thoughts and feelings. It's a small move out of unconscious behaviour and into conscious behaviour. Stepping back into awareness provides a small gap where we can notice our thoughts and feelings, and instead of just going along with them and the habitual patterns of our life, we can make a choice to act in a different way.

That's what was happening with me. I've had a life-long pattern of being passive with romantic partners because of fear – despite identifying as being a strong, independent woman. For years, I didn't even see that this was happening, except in retrospect. Now, I can see it happening in action and make different choices in the moment. That's how we take our yoga off the mat and into our relationships and into our life. It's just awareness and conscious choice, it's never too early (or late) in our yoga journey to start.

The best place to practice this level of awareness is... on the yoga mat. That's why it's called yoga practice. It's the place where we hone our ability to observe our experience and be non-reactive to it.

We observe that we're in pigeon pose and we feel like screaming and running away – and we don't. We come back to our breath and keep ourselves steady and watch those thoughts and feelings slowly dissipate and fade, and still we're there in the posture.

However, it's all too easy to build up this great yoga practice on the mat and never realise that it also needs to come off the mat.

You might be able to do the most amazing Scorpion Pose ever, but if the yoga isn't affecting your character and how you interact with life, there's a major disconnect going on.

That's why asana is only one of the eight limbs of Yoga. It's an entry point and a valuable one, but it's not the be all and end all.

The real benefits of yoga start to flow when you take your yoga off the mat.

Home yoga practice: is it for me, I've just started!?

You may have yet to walk into your first yoga class, so the idea of starting a home yoga practice seems crazy. Practice at home? But I don't even know any postures yet and I have no idea what I'm doing!

No, you don't. But that's okay. The big thing with home practice is that it doesn't matter so much what you do in your practice, it matters that you practice every day.

When we first start home practice, we're really building our ability to just show up to the mat every day; that's the most important thing. We soon learn that the mind has 101 reasons why we can't practice yoga today. We don't have enough time, we don't have the right space, we can't be bothered, or we don't know what to do... there's always a reason. This doesn't change either – I've been practicing yoga at home for over a decade now and there's still always something else I could be doing other than getting on my mat, or some reason why I can't possibly practice yoga today.

Over time though, I've learned that no matter what the reason, it's just an excuse and there's always a work-around. There's always some way you can get yoga practice in.

I've written an entire book on the subject, *Forty Days of Yoga – Breaking down the barriers to a home yoga practice*. That's where

4. Your Yoga Practice

you can find everything you need to know about creating and maintaining a home yoga practice, including handy worksheets.

All you need to know right now is that it's never too early to start practicing at home. In fact, I highly recommend that right from your very first yoga class, you start practicing yoga at home. There are a few reasons for this.

Reason #1

You're sending a message to yourself that yoga is important to you and you're going to give it your best shot. It's not just a way to escape from your life once a week on the mat, but something you intend to integrate into your life.

Reason #2

Taking time to go over just one thing that you learned in class will fast-track your understanding of yoga so when you do show up to that class every week, you'll get so much more out of it.

Reason #3

Doing some yoga at home by yourself means you're taking responsibility for your practice. It's not something that the teacher hands down to you every week, but something that you take responsibility for learning in your own time. This is an important step towards empowerment.

Reason #4

You'll feel better every time you practice yoga at home. It's like a small pick-me-up in the middle of your day. If you're having a really bad day – and we all have those – you know you can just get on your mat for five minutes of practice and things may just shift. Your perspective may broaden and suddenly whatever is bugging you might not be as bad.

120

Reason #5

Right from the start of your yoga journey, you're imprinting home yoga practice into your nervous system and your psyche. It makes yoga a way of life for you and means that you'll get so much more out of your practice.

I could keep going – I'm passionate about home practice and believe that every yoga practitioner could benefit from practicing at home, as well as going to yoga classes.

In the end, your yoga practice is your own individual journey and taking time by yourself on your mat gives you the space to really connect with what's going on in your body, mind and with your breath.

Now, before you freak out and think that a home yoga practice means doing this spectacular ninety minute sequence of postures every day, take a deep breath in and feel that breath as it fills your nostrils, then your lungs, and descends down into your belly. Release that breath and feel as the body softens and surrenders as it expels the breath. That moment? Watching your breath? Becoming conscious of what it feels like and sounds like in your body. *That* was yoga. You were present and conscious of your breath. Congratulations. You just did some home yoga practice.

When you first start going to yoga class, it is enough to take five or seven minutes every day doing just one posture that you remember. Perhaps you choose Shavasana (Corpse Pose), which is traditionally done at the end of every yoga class.

In Shavasana you lie flat on your back, legs hip-width, releasing your feet out sideways, palms facing up to the ceiling and away from the sides of your body. Eyes closed, tongue released from the roof of your mouth; and you breathe. And you continue breathing while staying conscious of your breath.

The mind will wander: 'Oh I wonder what I should cook for dinner tonight, I can't believe my sister is still dating that guy, I have to call the plumber tomorrow. Oh!' And then you notice it's wandering and you come back to your breath again letting those thoughts go. Inhale. Exhale.

Hmm... 'I need to buy a card for my mother's birthday...' And so it goes on. Just doing this every day between classes is a home yoga practice. It's a great place to start. In fact, given the nature of many of our lives – busy, busy, busy, online all the time, commuting – our nervous systems are over-stimulated and we need the stillness of Shavasana more than even the dynamism of Sun Salutations.

You may feel like you're not doing anything – you're just lying on the ground, watching your mind and your breath – but that's the whole point. Most of us spend all of our days doing, doing, doing and often our yoga practice becomes just another thing to DO. Taking time for Shavasana every day is taking time to be – nothing to do, nothing to achieve, nothing to attain, nothing to perfect, nothing to fix or heal or change. Just us, our breath and our body.

Other simple and effective postures you may wish to explore are Child's Pose, or Mountain Pose, or one of my favourites, Legs up the Wall Pose. If you can't remember exactly how to do the postures, Google it, read through, watch a video, get it clear in your head, and then get on your mat and practice that posture.

The beauty of taking time to do your own home practice right from Day 1 of yoga is that when you go back to class, you may have a question you want to ask the teacher, because you've spent time in the posture and are beginning to notice things about your body. Plus, an experienced teacher will be able to tell you're doing a home yoga practice. Students who practice at home progress so much faster than students who don't. Not that yoga is about progress as such, but it's obvious who is practicing at home as the yoga deepens into those students' bodies faster.

So even if you haven't yet made it to your first yoga class, know that you can start practicing yoga at home straight away. It doesn't have to be fancy and it doesn't have to be long. Mostly, you're focusing on building the habit of integrating yoga into your life and the habit of taking responsibility for your practice – of paying attention to your body and mind and observing what's actually going on. It's simple, but it's powerful.

That's yoga.

5. CHOOSING TEACHERS, CLASSES & STUDIOS

Yoga styles: finding your fit

It's no wonder that people new to yoga or people contemplating yoga get so confused and flummoxed. There are styles upon styles upon styles upon styles of yoga to choose from and new ones being born every day.

But, yoga is yoga is yoga. That's the first thing. Remember, yoga is the practice, the path and the destination. All of which is a state of being. Yoga is *presence*. Forget about asking which style is better or which style is real yoga.

The only question you need to concern yourself with is: which style works for me right now? Which style works for my body, brings me into a state of presence and makes me a kinder and more compassionate human being?

The second thing you need to remember is those four paths of yoga – Raja, Jnana, Bhakti and Karma.

They're all yoga, but physical styles of yoga fall under one path – Raja; and physical yoga is called Hatha. All physical styles of yoga – whether it's Bikram, Power, Hot, Prana Flow, AcroYoga or Stand-Up Paddle Board Yoga – it's all Hatha Yoga, which is a part of Raja Yoga.

Back in the 1950s and 1970s when Hatha Yoga was first introduced to the West, it was either just called Yoga or it was called

Hatha. Now, you'll still see Hatha Yoga listed on some studio timetables or community classes as a style, which is different from Hatha Yoga as all physical forms of Yoga. But not so different – you could say Hatha Yoga is just Yoga that was never claimed or created by one person in particular.

Now that's clear as mud, let's look at some of the major styles of Hatha Yoga, where they came from and what they're like. Where appropriate, we'll look at some of the lineages and connect the dots.

Let's start with the godfather of yoga in the West, Krishnamacharya. He instructed Iyengar – for only a year – who went on to teach Iyengar Yoga, and became one of the most well-known yoga teachers of the 20th Century. Supporters are now suggesting that Iyengar be nominated for a Nobel Peace Prize.

Iyengar Yoga is noted for its precise alignment and the number of props used to support students in postures – blocks, straps, sandbags, benches and ropes. It can be a good style for beginners because the nuances of each posture are fully explained and there is far more time to find your way into each pose.

Krishnamacharya also taught Pattabhi Jois who taught Ashtanga Vinyasa Yoga – six series of postures that Krishnamacharya developed for the young, athletic men he was working with at the time (back in the 1930s).

Ashtanga Yoga as it's usually shortened to, uses the sun salutation as its cornerstone and focuses on breath-led movement (vinyasa), bandhas (internal locks) and drishtis (gaze points).

It's physically challenging – not just for one's flexibility but also one's strength and fitness level. Ashtanga Yoga is often taught "Mysore-style", named after the town that Pattabhi Jois taught in and the way he taught. In Mysore classes, students show up and go through the set sequence at their own pace while the teacher and his or her assistants walk around instructing and adjusting students. Strict Mysore-style only allows students to progress in the sequence as the teacher sees that they're ready. In this way, the yoga – while a set sequence – is tailored for the needs of the individual.

Ashtanga Vinyasa Yoga has in turn birthed Power Yoga, which was 'created' by American Beryl Bender Birch. She wanted to make Ashtanga Yoga more accessible for an American audience so renamed it, and made minor changes to the sequence as well, simplifying it.

Ashtanga Vinyasa Flow has also morphed into Vinyasa Flow, taught by teachers like Shiva Rea and Baron Baptiste. While a Vinyasa Flow class draws heavily on sun salutations and flowing from posture to posture with the breath just like Ashtanga, classes are not set sequences and will vary from teacher to teacher and class to class. There's also more variety on offer with some teachers including chanting, pranayama and more meditation in the class mix. Vinyasa is often taught to music.

Another Ashtanga child is Jivamukti Yoga, co-founded in 1986 by David Life and Sharon Gannon. They took the vinyasa style approach of Ashtanga Yoga, but added other elements including chanting, readings, affirmations, meditations and music.

T.K.V. Desikachar, Krishnamacharya's son, created Viniyoga, which is a gentler asana practice based on the needs of the individual and the time of their life.

These many spin-offs from one man – Krishnamacharya – is why he's often called the Godfather of Modern Yoga.

Another major lineage to have an impact on Western Yoga is that of Bishnu Ghosh – younger brother of Yogananda, author of *Autobiography of a Yogi*. Bishnu was one of the first students to enrol at Yogananda's Ranchi School for Boys, where he learned the Yogoda system – including 84 classical asana. In turn Bishnu Ghosh taught these 84 Classical Asana to Bikram who, after spending time in a Japanese Hospital researching the healing effects of the asana, created a 26 posture sequence designed to work with beginning Western bodies. That sequence became Bikram Yoga, and Bikram has worked hard to keep it pure and unadulterated, going as far as to sue people for teaching his sequence without using the Bikram Yoga name.

However, other former students have still taken the Bikram Sequence and evolved it according to their needs and the needs of their students. Hot Yoga is one clear example – it often combines the sun salutations of Ashtanga Vinyasa Yoga with the postures of Bikram Yoga and the heat of the Bikram room.

Other breakaways from Bikram include Tony Sanchez and Evolation Yoga. Tony Sanchez has gone back to drawing from all 84 classical asanas in his classes, and Evolation includes other elements like meditation in their classes.

Other styles of Hatha Yoga include Sivananda Yoga, which was created by the disciples of Swami Sivananda. Incidentally, Swami Sivananda was the guru of Swami Satyananda (Satyananda Yoga) and Swami Satchidanda (Integral Yoga). The purpose of Sivanada Yoga is self-realisation – Who am I? Really, that's the purpose of all yoga, including Hatha Yoga and all styles – even Bikram. But some styles put that purpose front and centre, and use practices like asana to then attain that. Other more physical styles put the asana front and centre and allow any kind of self-realisation to just "happen". Sivanada Yoga teaches only 12 basic asana, plus chanting, meditation and pranayama.

Kundalini Yoga is another style that crosses the divide – it was introduced by Yogi Bhajan, a turban-wearing Sikh swami clad only in white. Kundalini Yoga descends from Tantra Yoga – no, that doesn't mean it's all about sex! Tantra simply means 'teaching' and is all about self-realisation through the practice of kriyas or complex meditations.

Kundalini Yoga uses kriyas – techniques designed to achieve a specific result. For example, you might learn a heart-opening kriya. This kriya includes seven different exercises, two of which include a specific pranayama. Kriyas will also use meditation, visualisation, mudras and chanting. The focus in Kundalini Yoga is on creating awareness through which you experience your soul. For absolute beginners, the practice can seem weird and strange, because it's not so much about moving the body or holding poses. However, it's can also be energetically powerful and have some strong effects.

This might be a yoga style that's been and gone already, burned out in the flames of its creator's demise – Anusara Yoga. Created by former marketing guru John Friend, Anusara is (was?) an alignment-based style (John Friend came from Iyengar) that focuses on opening to 'grace'. Exactly what opening to grace means... I'm not sure. Unfortunately, merits of the style aside, the fall from grace of its founder means Anusara has also fallen on hard times.

Restorative Yoga is as its name sounds – there to restore you. Like Iyengar, it uses lots of props, but those props are mostly to support you in the postures as you recline and let go with long holds. The idea is to make the postures completely passive so you can lie there and surrender into the pose without having to exert yourself physically at all. Restorative can be great for a person with injuries, but it's also good for those of us with stressed nervous systems and too much go go go in our lives.

Yin Yoga is also a softer style of yoga that allows more time to surrender into the postures. It was founded by Paulie Zink in the late 1970s and has its roots in China – Paulie is also a Martial Arts Grand Champion. In a Yin class, you hold postures for three minutes or more, and some can even be held for ten minutes or longer. Yin Yoga is complementary to more Yang styles of Yoga like Power Yoga. You may do three Power Classes in a week, and then finish up with a Yin Class to balance your body out and allow more surrender, letting go and release. You could say that Yin isn't so much a style as a way to approach the yoga. Yin Yoga's relative passivity allows muscles to relax, with the use of props, into long holds so that the practitioner can work on releasing connective tissue and fascia. Strong sensations and feelings can come up as you work into releasing parts of your body that have never let go before. That means Yin can be more challenging psychologically – it's like a deep cleansing for the psyche.

Aside from authoring over 80 books including *Asana Pranayama Mudra Bandha*, Swami Satyananda Saraswati also founded Satyananda Yoga. This approach to yoga is grounded in Tantra. Asana is but one of its components, and it has a strong emphasis on other elements of yoga including Kirtan (chanting) and Karma Yoga. If you go to a Satyananda-trained teacher, you can expect a class with moderate asana, plus a focus on pranayama, chanting and meditation. Sometimes there is also a talk to end the class that discusses elements of yoga philosophy. Satyananda also bought Yoga Nidra into the 20th Century, based on his study of ancient Tantric texts.

Finally, there are the newer hybrid styles of yoga that have appeared in the last ten years:

- Acro-Yoga: Yoga with a partner where one person acts as the 'base', and the other person perches on top of them. Together you move through a variety of yoga postures.
- Aerial Yoga: Suspended a few feet above the ground in a specially designed hammock, students are taken through aerial moves with the support of the fabric.
- SUP Yoga: Yoga on a Stand-Up Paddle Board... body of water essential!
- Laughter Yoga: Yep – it focuses on getting you to laugh...

By no means exhaustive, this list gives you a broad idea of the many styles of yoga out there. Don't feel overwhelmed by the choices. The styles tend to group together nicely.

There are the more physically-demanding styles that mostly came from Ashtanga Vinyasa Yoga including Astanga, Power, Jivamukti and Vinyasa.

There's alignment-based styles like Iyengar and Anusara.

There's softer styles like Hatha Yoga (not always softer, but tends to be), Viniyoga, Restorative and Yin.

There are the hot styles including Bikram, Hot Yoga and yoga from former Bikram Teachers like Tony Sanchez and Evolation Yoga.

Finally, there are the styles of yoga which while they include asana, don't focus on it so much. Their aim is self-realisation, front and centre. That's Kundalini, Sivananda, and Satyananda, These styles address the whole of the individual and allow for more discussion on the deeper elements of yoga.

Often though, the deciding element on what style of yoga to do is convenience. Which styles are available to you? Beyond that, it comes down to the teacher. If you go to an Iyengar class with a terrible teacher and a Bikram class with an awesome teacher... you're going to think Bikram Yoga rocks.

When you first start yoga, if you do have many different styles and teachers available to you, I would suggest trying as many classes as possible. Find out what's out there, and choose one style or teacher to commit to. Stick with that teacher or style for at least a year and really get to know that particular style of yoga.

Overtime, you may switch it up and move to a different style, but often the real benefits of practice don't unfold until we take time to go over and over and over the same territory. Flitting from one thing to the next and then the next, we often miss out on the depths of the practice.

Remember too that this chapter has focused on the styles of Hatha Yoga – and there are other ways to practice yoga out there. Yoga is a big wide world!

How to find a great yoga teacher

'How do I find a good yoga teacher?' you ask. How indeed?

First, start by defining what a good yoga teacher means to you, as it will be different for everyone

What values and factors matter to you? What do you want in a teacher? Things you might want to consider include:

- location
- price
- skill set
- training
- style

- age
- gender
- attributes (kind, stern, funny...)
- experience

For example, if you've never done yoga before and you have a limited budget but plenty of time your ideal yoga teacher may be an old-school experienced community teacher working a few suburbs away from you. The price is cheap, you don't mind travelling to get there, and the teacher is welcoming and supportive of beginners.

If you're an experienced yoga practitioner and you want someone to take you to the next level, your ideal yoga teacher will be highly experienced, actively learning and training, and teaching classes tailored to more experienced students.

If you've got a specific injury that you want to use yoga to address, you'll be looking for a teacher with experience of yoga therapy who is available for one-on-one work.

Once you're clear on exactly what kind of yoga teacher you're looking for, then you can start the search.

It always pays to know what you're looking for before you go looking right?

Start by asking anyone you know who practices yoga in your area – who do they recommend, who do they go to, and who have they heard good things about?

Check out any local publications and see who advertises there – newspapers, newsletters, magazines. Keep an eye out on the noticeboards in your local area, especially in health food stores, libraries, alternative stores or local colleges.

Do a google search using your location and variations of yoga classes/yoga teacher. See what comes up.

Once you've compiled a list of potential yoga teachers, classes and studios you're ready for the next step. Using all those different sources, compare the results to your list. Who looks or sounds like they might match up?

Find the bios or the 'About' pages of teachers on their website and read them. Bear in mind that some of the best yoga teachers may not be on the Internet at all – those are the teachers you find via word of mouth.

Once you've got a list of teachers or classes that match your list of what you want, narrow it down to three or so teachers.

Call each of those teachers and have a chat to them. Ask them what their classes are like. Let them know what you're looking for in particular (help with an injury, to deepen your practice, get stronger, lose weight or start yoga for the first time).

Ask your top three yoga teachers about their own practice, who they trained with and what certifications they've got. Ask them how long they've been practicing yoga, how long they've had a home practice, what their home practice is like, and how long they've been teaching yoga.

Listen to the response – that's the most important thing! And while you're listening to the response, notice how you're responding – not so much in your mind, but in your body. Tune into your own intuition.

Sometimes the teacher that sounds and looks good in marketing material is not the best teacher for you.

Based on your short list and those conversations, choose a class to go to. Take a friend if you can. It can be really useful to have someone else's input, and support when you're going to a brand new yoga class.

When you go to class, pay attention to the *important* things and forget about the rest.

The room is best if it's warm or cool enough, dry and clean with good light. Beyond that, fancy fittings don't really matter. What does matter is the teacher.

- Do you get to meet them before class?
- Do they ask you about your experience level and body?
- How do they address the class when they start?
- Do they create a safe space for people to explore?
- Is the class challenging but accessible?
- Do you feel better after class?
- Is the teacher available after class to answer any questions you may have?

At its very best, a yoga experience is a shared relationship between a teacher and student.

Over time, you will be able to cultivate a relationship with your teacher that supports your practice. But it's your responsibility as a student to tell the teacher anything you think might impact your practice. If your teacher is to keep you safe, full disclosure is necessary!

In fact, it's really important that if you have any specific health issues – high blood pressure, fused discs or the like, that you tell the teacher well before class – maybe in that initial phone call.

It's important that the teacher knows what that means and how to modify the postures for you. Ideally, if you have a specific issue, it's a good idea to talk to the teacher before you come to class so your teacher has time to talk to you about what that means in class and prepare you for any modifications.

In the end, a good yoga teacher is knowledgeable, thorough, kind, caring, patient and knows how to take care of you.

The *best* teachers will also gently push you in the right direction, beyond your comfort zone. They will *see* you – truly see you – behind the mask of ego you wear. This can be uncomfortable because they may challenge you on some of your comfort behaviours – like having to always have the same spot for your yoga mat. You may find that sometimes, you don't even like them. That's okay – as long as they respect your boundaries and help to keep you safe.

If you follow these steps, and bring full awareness and attention to the process as you do (that's yoga right there), you will find the yoga teacher that is right for you.

You'll just know.

And if you don't, keep looking, they're out there somewhere. It took me over a decade to find a teacher I really wanted to work with. In that time, I was going to yoga classes sporadically, with some good teachers, but none who I really wanted to study with. Then I met Peter Sanson – an Ashtanga teacher. I'm not an Ashtangi yogi at all, but after doing three Mysore-style classes with him, I made the decision to move across the country so I could regularly attend his classes. (Mysore-style classes are not led – you show up and do your own practice (the Ashtanga sequence) and the teacher comes around and gives you adjustments). I'd long given up finding a teacher I could work with – yet right from that first class I knew that Peter was the one for me. What made him different?

First, the most important aspect for me was that he could see I was holding all this tension in my body that wasn't really 'me'. He didn't see me as naturally tight or rigid or stuck or injured. He saw me as a flowing open person who happened to be blocking herself by holding tension in her body. A yoga teacher that truly sees you is worth gold.

Secondly, Peter has been seriously studying Ashtanga for decades and spent twenty odd years travelling to India to study directly with his teacher, Pattabhi Jois. That meant he had the kind of depth I needed. Yoga practice takes time to work its way into the body and psyche. Teachers can only really teach out of their own experience, and as I had 15 years of practice under my belt, I needed a teacher who was far beyond that. Plus, a teacher that has spent serious time working with another highly experienced teacher is just going to know more. Yoga takes time to develop in a person – I can't stress that highly enough.

Thirdly, I felt like I could trust Peter, and he had a strict but kind and compassionate way about him. I knew he wouldn't let me bullshit him in any way, but he would share whatever truth he saw with kindness and compassion. I felt held and supported in his classes. This is also crucial – yoga can bring up all kinds of things emotionally, and in the psyche. You need to work with a teacher who can hold the space of class in such a way that you are safe – that no matter what comes up, you feel supported.

So when you're looking for a yoga teacher – remember there are two kinds. There's the kind that will teach a good class and give you a good practice. I've had plenty of these over the years and have always been grateful for what I've learned from them. Then there's the teacher who sees you clearly and will help you take your practice to the next level.

They always say, when the student is ready the teacher will appear. For years, I doubted that, and was beginning to think it was a load of crap. After all, I'd been looking for a decade and surely I was ready! Yet maybe I wasn't...

If you can't find the perfect teacher for you, make do with the good enough teacher. That will be good enough, for now.

How to choose the right yoga studio for you

Choosing the right yoga studio is much like choosing the right yoga teacher. It's about getting clear on what you want to experience, doing some research and then going to studios to check them out.

However, while that can sound simple, it's not always easy. Even when we know exactly what we want and we've done our research, it can be intimidating to walk into a new studio for the first time. You're venturing into the unknown.

So be prepared to face some discomfort and fear. But to help lessen that discomfort and fear, here are a few tips to get you off the procrastination flow and into the yoga flow.

1. Ask yourself what you're looking for

If you don't know what you want, how are you going to recognise it when you see it? Before you even look up studios or talk to people about studios, take some time to write down exactly what kind of studio you want to go to. What matters in a studio to you?

Some of the factors you may want to consider include:

- Location
- Yoga Styles on Offer
- Schedule and times on offer
- Pricing
- Facilities available – lockers, childcare, showers, free parking, cafe
- Decor
- Views
- Yoga shop
- Library/ resources
- Sense of Community
- Social Buzz

Imagine yourself going to this studio, walking in the front door, being greeted at reception, going into the changing rooms, getting changed and storing your belongings, going into the yoga room, practicing, coming out and showering and/or getting changed, and leaving.

What does that experience look like for you? What does it feel like? Do you just dash in and do your thing, and get out? Or is it like stepping into a second home where everybody knows your name and you might hang out after class and chat to people?

Take that experience and write it out. If I was doing this exercise, here's what I would write. Yes, it's my ideal yoga studio and I may not find everything on my list, but at least now I'm clear about what matters to me.

I park my car within five minutes walk of the studio – there's always space and it doesn't cost anything. The reception area is spacious, with books to browse and places to sit and chat before or after class. The receptionist or teacher usually remembers my name and has time to chat. The changing rooms are light and airy, with three shower stalls. There's lockers provided. The yoga room comfortably fits about 40 people and is light and airy with natural views – lake, mountain, trees and the like. There are mirrors along one wall that can be lit up or turned off, depending on the style of the class. Props are easily available, and there's a great sound system. Class usually has between 10 – 40 people, and in the big classes there will be two teachers – one taking the lead and one assisting students where necessary. The teacher always makes themselves available after class for about ten minutes to answer any questions. You're welcome to hang out in reception afterwards and browse the yoga library or chat with other students. Good sound-proofing means you never disturb the yoga class underway. There's always a class on the schedule for 9:30am, so I can drop my child at school and catch a class before getting stuck into work.

Your dream yoga studio may be completely different to mine – but it's not until you write it out that you'll know exactly what it is you're looking for.

2. Now that you're clear on what you want, it's time to do some research

Start with the people you know – maybe even though social media. Post a question asking what studio people go to in your home town and why? This can often be the fastest way to find out anything – it's easy to get a lively discussion going. If people tag the studios they're talking about, social-media savvy studios may even respond to your post as well.

You can always go the old-fashioned route and talk to friends and family – get recommendations that way. Check out your local newspaper and notice-boards to find out what studios are operating in your area – or try Google. Remember, even though we live in a digital age, not every studio is online and sometimes the ones that aren't are well worth hunting down.

3. Talk to the studios

Once you know what you want, go and check the studios out in person – you don't have to go to class, just drop-in to do a tour of the facilities. Make sure you call ahead to find out the best time to do this, as many studios lock their doors during class, and are often closed between classes.

Pay attention to how you feel when you walk into each studio, and the way you are treated.

Are you listened to? Are you attended to quickly? Do you feel good in the studio? Ask for a tour of the facilities. Check out the decor – what's on the walls? Do other students say hi in passing? Take away a timetable or any marketing material so you can study it.

4. Work out what times will suit you, and what budget works for you

Sometimes the studio or teacher we choose comes down to convenience, so it helps to know when you would be likely to go to class and how much a class is worth to you.

Don't think of the money you spend on a class as the same as spending money on entertainment, think of it as investment in your health and well-being. A regular yoga practice can help rehabilitate injuries and prevent new ones, and can also provide relief from certain conditions, and prevent new conditions from developing. How much is your health worth to you?

But do be mindful in committing to an annual membership when you've never done that style of yoga before. Try starting with a beginners' offer – most studios will offer some kind of deal for your first few classes. Or try a ten class pass. Then, when you know what you really love, dive in and get the best deal by committing to a year.

5. Try, try and try again

The best time to think about joining a studio is when it first opens, because usually they will offer free yoga for a period of time so you can check out the classes, and they often offer discounted joining specials.

So jump in and try as many classes as you can, with different teachers and different styles until you find something you like. You may discover you love classical Hatha Yoga, but the teacher doesn't quite speak your language, so find another teacher – or try a different studio. It's okay to try three or four studios before you finally commit to one. Even then, some people go to a couple of studios at a time because of the teachers, styles, and times on offer.

Right now, I'm attending Mysore-style Astanga with Peter Sanson three times a week and going to Bikram occasionally. I get something different out of each experience.

Each teacher brings something different to a class, and appeals to different people. Just because your friend raves about a particular teacher, it doesn't mean you too will love him or her. Which leads onto...

6. *Pay attention to the teacher*

If you've never done yoga before, it's hard to know what a great yoga teacher is like, compared to a not-so-great yoga teacher, because you have nothing to compare against. Each teacher will have a different style too. Some teachers like to physically adjust and correct their students, while other teachers prefer to give verbal corrections and adjustments and let the students find the pose from within.

Regardless of their style though, what great teachers all have in common is that they 'see' their students. They notice when alignment needs correcting, and when breathing is strained. They see where students are tight, and where they are weak.

A great teacher is responsive to the needs of their class, and doesn't recite the instructions for each asana by rote, instead paying attention to what needs to be said in that moment – even in Bikram, which is known for its tightly scripted class. A great Bikram teacher can work with the script, and still be responsive to the needs of individual students.

If, after trying a smattering of styles and teachers, yoga still doesn't grab you... then maybe it's not for you at this point in life. But don't write it off for good – we change every year, and yoga is such a transformative practice, you may find that down the track, it does appeal to you. Think beyond asana – maybe what you're looking for is meditation or chanting or even the study of yogic texts.

It's all too easy to get hung up on convenience or shiny extras – oh that studio is right next to my work or that studio has a sauna in the changing rooms... but if the styles of yoga on offer aren't right for you or you don't connect with the teacher, you're better off finding a different studio, convenience or not, sauna or not.

Yoga etiquette: the do's & don'ts of yoga classes

Entering a yoga studio or a yoga class for the very first time can be an intimidating experience.

Everybody else looks so confident and relaxed and sure of themselves. They're all stronger and fitter and leaner and bendier than you – or at least it seems that way.

But every single person in that room was once a beginner – including the teacher. What you're seeing is likely the *result* of yoga – there's been a lot of learning going on and a lot of practicing. Me? When I started yoga, I couldn't bend forward and reach my knees, let alone my toes.

Yoga is all about practice and learning – some of which takes place outside of the class and off the mat.

After all, there's no reason why you can't learn a few things before you head into your first class, because that's going to make you feel more confident, more relaxed and more sure of yourself.

If you are going to a Bikram Class, there's nothing wrong with researching the class sequence and finding a visual of the postures so you know what you're in for. Ditto if you're going to an Ashtanga class. If you going to a Vinyasa Flow class, guaranteed there'll be some sun salutations in there. Watch a YouTube video and at least get an idea of the flow.

Prepare yourself as best you can so you feel more comfortable. Talk to friends, read books, watch YouTube.

Here's a few other tips on Yoga Etiquette that will make you feel more comfortable about going to class.

Turning Up

Show up at least fifteen minutes early to your first class as you can expect to fill in a registration form plus you want time to meet the teacher.

Wear comfortable clothes that are tight enough so when you're upside down in downward dog, your t-shirt doesn't fall down around your neck. There's nothing worse than having to keep yanking your t-shirt up as it falls across your eyes yet again.

Legs also go upside down and wide, so wear pants that don't gape – baggy shorts just don't work in yoga, especially for men.

Don't wear tops that are too low in front either. You're often bending forward and what looks modest standing up in your bedroom may look come-hither in the yoga room.

If you're doing a hot class, it's okay to wear very little clothing – some people even just wear a swimsuit in some studios – but that clothing still needs to be modest and well fitting. You don't want your butt hanging out in people's faces or your boobs flashing either.

Yoga is always done in bare feet so expect to take your socks off.

When you enter the room, do so quietly and be mindful of the people around you who may be lying in Shavasana. Always lay your mat out with the minimum of movement, keeping it quiet. No slapping the mat down jolting the person beside you who's chilling out or drifting off into Bliss.

Bring a warmer layer for Shavasana – the relaxation normally done at the end of class.

Water is not a big thing for most yoga classes – except those in heated rooms. Do come hydrated though! Drink plenty beforehand.

Don't eat two hours before class – those weird bendy shapes do funny things to your insides as well as your outsides.

Introduce yourself to the teacher, say hi and ask them any questions you may have. A good teacher should be available beforehand to connect with students. But sometimes, it does get crazy busy and the teacher might be dealing with a 101 last minute issues. If so, make time to have a chat to the teacher after class.

On the mat

Pick a student that looks like they know what they're doing and use them as a visual reference.

Choose a spot nearer the back of the room where you can still see the teacher, but you can also follow the more experienced students in front.

Stagger your mat with your neighbour so when you stretch your arms out wide you don't whack into their arms.

Always be aware of where you are on the mat – top? Middle? Back? That way when you have to suddenly jump your feet back, there's mat behind you!

Never, ever push into pain. If it hurts, back off. If the teacher pushes you or pulls you and it doesn't feel right, let them know right away! Some styles have stronger tendencies, but it's your body and trust it when it hurts – that's not a good sign and you need to back off.

Yoga is not about being bendy, it's not about being strong, it's not about looking a certain way – it's all about being present. We get present by listening to our breath. It's the number one thing in class. So don't worry too much about whether or not you're doing the pose 'right', focus your awareness on your breath. Can you hear yourself breathing? Is your breath steady and firm? Are you holding your breath?

Once you are present and you can maintain your awareness on your breath, you will find it's easier to move in and out of postures – ultimately in time, your breath will effortlessly guide you in and out of the poses.

Never give up! If it gets hard or you need a break or you feel sick or you suddenly want to burst into tears... get down on the mat in Child's Pose. A good teacher should always tell you this before class and show you what Child's Pose looks like. Once you're in Child, just breathe and watch whatever's going on inside of you – thoughts, feelings, sensations... breathe and watch.

Other people

Forget about all the other people in the room!

They don't care what you're doing, what you look like, what you're wearing, or if you just farted. And if they do care, that's their issue, not yours. Tune them out and tune into your breath.

If your mind is racing with lots of thoughts along the lines of 'You'll never be able to do this, this was a bad idea, you're the tightest in the room, you suck...' Well forget about it! Those thoughts don't matter, you don't have to listen to your mind anymore. You're here to listen to your breath and be right where you are today. If that is tight as all hell, well then that's okay! Just notice those thoughts and keep letting them go. If it helps, talk back to your mind as if you were a life coach. 'You're just a beginner, it's okay to be the tightest person in the room, it's okay to suck, you will get better, just keep breathing.'

Remember, no one has any expectations of you, nor do they know what's going on inside of you. Yoga is about your practice. If you find yourself watching other people, bring your awareness back to your breath and to your internal experience. Do it over and over and over again – as many times as it takes to stay focused on yourself. You are the only person in the room that matters.

Faux pas in class

If you fart or burp or make some other weird noises, it's okay. You don't need to apologise, or explain, or laugh hysterically to cover your nerves. Yes, you may feel embarrassed or ashamed – challenge yourself to just allow those feelings to be there and let them go. Stay with your breath and in your flow. Stay focused.

Some classes are really close to each other, so if you bump up against another person, it's okay. Again, you don't have to apologise or say anything. Just stay focused and in your flow. See if you can adjust your movement slightly so it doesn't happen again.

If the person in front of you is wearing see-through pants or a low top or baggy shorts that reveal too much, keep your eyes down and on a drishti (gaze point) within your own sphere. Stare at the edge of your mat or the wall or the ceiling – depending on which pose you're in and where your eyes are meant to be going naturally. Resist the urge to keep staring at the flesh on display.

If you have intense emotions come up and feel like crying, it's okay to do this. Most people will discretely take themselves into something like Child's Pose where the head is down and it's possible to cry all the emotion out without disturbing the class too much. If you've mastered the art of crying silently, you can keep going through the postures letting the tears stream down your face. That's okay too. I've done it a few times. Forward bends are also a great refuge for tears, but it depends where you are in a class flow.

If you have a cold, make sure you take some tissues in with you so you can blow your nose if necessary. Sniffing all the way through class isn't nice for the people around you.

After class

After class has finished, generally move silently and gently as you exit the room – no talking in the room at all. Once you're outside the room, be aware that sound can carry in a yoga studio, so don't start cracking it up in the hallway or changing rooms.

If you used a studio mat, sometimes they like you to spray and wipe it down before hanging it up to dry. Sometimes they ask you to leave it flat and they do it for you.

If you've been using props, making sure you put them away, folding everything neatly and placing it with care.

If you have questions, sometimes the teacher will invite questions after class in the room, sometimes outside of the room. Be mindful of other students and see where the best place to speak to the teacher is.

Also be respectful of the teacher's time – generally yoga teachers don't get paid very much money and tying them up for half an hour after class with in-depth questions about the nature of your health condition isn't cool. Instead, if you need some one-on-one time with a teacher, book the time in and do a private session. You'll be amazed at how much you can get out of one private session with a skilled teacher.

Mostly, yoga etiquette can be summed up in two words – be aware. What's going on around you? What is everybody else doing? What does everybody else need? What do you need? It's learning to be sensitive to the system within which you move. Don't be afraid to ask if you don't know. If it's your first time, other students are usually more than happy to help you out.

Danger signs: how to keep yourself sexually safe

There are great teachers, there are good teachers, there are bad teachers and then there are criminal teachers – literally.

Some teachers end up in court because of their behaviour with students. Some just end up disgraced. The list of gurus and yoga teachers who have betrayed the trust of their students is long, predominantly male and compromised of both Indian and Western teachers.

For example, in 2013 five women filed civil suits against Bikram Choudhury for charges ranging from rape to sexual assault.* Also

---

* telegraph.co.uk/news/worldnews/northamerica/usa/10498946/Yoga-guru-Bikram-Choudhury-raped-students-in-cult-like-training-camps.html

in 2013, four women laid charges with Austrian police against Krishnamacharya's grandson, Kausthub, alleging sexual, mental and emotional abuse*. Plus in early 2013, John Friend was accused of abuse of power and philandering, among other things.†

This is nothing new in the yoga world. There have been many scandals over the years as gurus and teacher abuse their powers, dupe their students and disappoint their followers.

A wise yoga student knows all this history and realises that regardless of their teaching skills or apparent enlightenment, yoga teachers and gurus are human and fallible. They have both their light and their dark, and they too can succumb to the ego.

It's wise to always retain your common sense, ask questions, be sceptical and if something just doesn't feel right... don't drink the koolaid.

It's all too easy, especially as a beginning student, to idolise your teacher, to put them on a pedestal, or to bow down before their greatness and pander to their every whim.

That can lead to danger.

It's always easy in hindsight to see all the warning signs that something was seriously amiss in any given inner circle or yoga community. However, when you're immersed in that culture, those signs are much harder to see. Especially because the faithful don't want to see those signs or acknowledge anything that might threaten the status quo.

In Bikram's case, very few teachers I've spoken to are surprised at the current allegations – which haven't been proven either way as of yet. They're either true or plausible based on the culture that has long surrounded Bikram Headquarters.

So what are the warning signs that something is amiss within a yoga community or with a particular teacher?

---

* yogadork.com/2012/10/01/kausthub-desikachar-krishnamacharyas-grandson-accused-of-sexual-mental-emotional-abuse/

† nymag.com/news/features/john-friend-yoga-2012-4

- If something makes you uncomfortable, it's worth questioning. Don't just assume it's because you're not enlightened enough yet, or have deep-seated issues you haven't worked on. Bikram is famous for making off-colour sexual remarks. That's a sign that something's not quite right, or at least that it is worth paying extra attention to what might be going on. Maybe he's deliberately trying to push buttons to show you your shit or maybe it's his shit coming up for all to see. Never stop questioning.

- If the style of adjustment makes you feel uncomfortable, speak up. It may be the norm in some yoga styles (Ashtanga in particular) to receive intense adjustments from teachers that help you work your way into the pose, but that doesn't mean you have to go along with it. It's your body and your mat and you can say no at any time.

There's hot debate in the yoga sphere about circulating photos of Pattabhi Jois giving adjustments to women that look.... dodgy. His supporters say they're innocent and focused on helping the woman attain the proper alignment in the posture, bandhas and all. They say it's a Western mind interpretation that colours his innocent adjustment with sexual connotations. His detractors say the adjustment is bullshit and he's just copping a feel whilst others say the photos are faked using Photoshop.[‡]

Who knows what's true?

What I do know is that when a teacher you look up to, admire and trust wants to do something with your body it's very easy to override your own internal guidance because you want to please, you want to be seen and you want to belong.

---

‡ yogadork.com/2010/12/09/good-touch-bad-touch-gurus-power-and-adjusting-vs-groping-on-the-yoga-mat/, *YogaDork*, December 9, 2010

You want to impress this highly respected teacher by dutifully agreeing with and going along with whatever they say and do. Anytime you're over-riding intuition, or your gut feeling, or your inner knowing, or the little angel that sits on your right shoulder... at least get a second opinion. Talk to someone else you respect and admire who's also a friend and colleague. Share your concerns and ask questions. Never doubt yourself or dismiss your internal guidance.

- If other teachers within the community have been leaving, ask questions. Many senior teachers have left Bikram because they disagreed with some of his teaching methods, or believed that the yoga could evolve. He's even sued some of them. Before the allegations about John Friend finally hit the airwaves, there were a rash of high-profile Anusara Teachers leaving the fold, although they didn't specify why exactly they were going their own way.

- If you're getting up close and cosy with a yoga community, ask questions about how it functions and who the other senior teachers are and how it's evolved as an organisation. Kripalu's guru Amrit Desari famously fell from grace in 1994 after it was revealed he'd had three affairs with devotees. That community went through an extraordinarily difficult time as they used that event not just to castigate and expel Desari, but to look more deeply at the community of the culture that allowed such a thing to happen over such a long time. Kripalu survived that experience and has gone from strength to strength in the last decade.

- If the teacher singles you out for special attention, asks you to stay after class, implies that you have a special connection, wants you to take care of personal business for them... ask questions. We all want to belong and we all want to believe that we're special. When this belonging is handed to us on a plate and we told of how special we are, it can be difficult to remain skeptical and discerning because we want so badly to be in this place. But who better to groom a willing supplicant for sexual abuse than a yoga teacher?

- If you find yourself attracted to your yoga teacher and that attraction seems to be reciprocated, tread carefully.

There's long been debate in the yoga community about whether or not teachers and students should get together. It's tricky territory. Yoga teachers are attractive people. It's not unusual to get crushes on your teachers. However it can be confusing to find out they reciprocate the crush. You can't be sure if you're actually interested in the person, or in the image of the person. And the teacher could be caught in the same trap – not sure if they're interested in you as a person, or the adulation they feel from you. It's flattering to have students falling at your feet.

If you're a student and the teacher asks you out on a date, you both need to be clear about what's going on. I have a close female friend who found herself attracted to a student. As their friendship developed, she was clear with him.

'I can either be your yoga teacher or I can be your partner. I can't be both.'

He chose her as his partner and they were together for nearly four years. There was no abuse in this instance because the boundaries were clearly laid out, and each participant had the same amount of power. It's the imbalance of power that shifts the equation.

If you're looking up to a teacher or see them as more than you, above you, better than you or even just different from you – there's a power imbalance. A wise teacher will sense this and not take advantage of it. Sometimes though, an unwise teacher will sense this and unconsciously use the power balance to their advantage. Just as in any relationship, the person with more power will often use it to their advantage, even if it's only unconsciously.

If you want to avoid sexually abusive or difficult situations maintain a high degree of awareness and inquire into your situation – just as you do when you're in yoga class.

Yet, paradoxically, remember that 99.9% of yoga teachers are never going to abuse their students in any way. It's only the rare few that do this. However, it's also important to point out that it does happen, as it's all too easy to look upon all teachers with rose-tinted glasses.

If you have any doubts or concerns, talk to someone you can trust. Never be afraid to speak up. Never doubt your own intuition. If something feels off... believe that it *is* off until you get proof it's not. If you know that you're more susceptible to abusive situations – if you've previously experienced abuse or have had abusive relationships, recognise that you are more at risk and do what you need to keep yourself safe.

Dealing with fear: everybody's intimidated going to their first class

I'd wager a bet that the reason thousands of people around the world have never gone to yoga – despite talking about wanting to go to yoga, despite knowing that yoga would be great for them, despite knowing that they'd love yoga – is fear.

Yes *fear*. It's scary walking into a brand new situation, especially when it involves our bodies, skimpy clothing, unfamiliar language and weird body shapes. Not only do we not really know what to expect, but we also have ideas about yoga that are wildly wrong, yet perfectly natural given the kind of yoga media most of us are exposed to.

Yoga is about lying around on the floor stretching. It's low-key, easy and old women do it. That was likely the impressions back in the 1970s and 1980s, and in some ways it wasn't that far from the truth. Yoga was more low-key back then, there was likely a lot of time spent on the floor and predominantly, it was older women who first embraced yoga.

However, yoga has changed. It's athletic and demanding, fast-paced and strong, and it often involves advanced pretzel poses – preferably done in one's underwear in a beautiful outdoor location. And yoga is predominantly made up of skinny white women in their early twenties. At least, that's what you'd think if you based your perception solely on yoga media and the current craze of the yoga selfie.

It's no wonder we feel intimated when we head into our first class. We don't know if we're flexible enough, we don't know if we're strong enough, we don't know if we're dressed right, we don't know if we'll be able to understand the teacher, we don't know anything at all.

It's like standing on the edge of a cliff blindfolded and being asked to step off. Who knows if you'll fly or not?

The first thing to realise about this fear is that it's natural and normal. Not only that – everybody has it. I even have it – despite practicing yoga for more than a decade and teaching for six or seven years. When I turn up to a new class, a new teacher or a weekend workshop, I feel nervous and intimidated and yes, even fearful.

The difference between you and I is that I'm observing this fear and nervousness inside of me, and I'm not identified with it. I'm still in a place of equanimity despite my fear and nervousness. Because of this, I can see that everyone else is nervous and afraid too. Maybe not to the same degree, but when we're all new at something – like a weekend workshop – everyone is unsure and unsettled on that first session.

So if you find yourself quivering in your boots if you even *think* about going to a yoga class, rest assured, you're not alone and it's normal. Here's what to do with that fear.

1. Find a friend

Oh the glory of shared fear and anxiety. Suddenly, it's not just you freaking out, you've got someone else to freak out with and that shared experience makes it all okay. You can cling to each other and giggle nervously as you find your way to the changing room and work out what props you need.

Having someone to share the experience with turns it into more of an adventure, where some nervousness and trepidation is expected.

2. Confide in the teacher or studio.

Maybe you can't find a friend, it is just you and you feel alone and afraid and nervous. When you sign up for the class tell the teacher or receptionist that it's your first time ever at yoga or your first time trying this style or your first time with this teacher or studio. Confide in the way you would if the teacher or receptionist was a close friend.

If they don't make you feel welcome when you reveal you're a newbie, you've just learned something important.

Maybe this isn't the teacher or studio for you. Don't let it put you off yoga and don't let it feed your fear or nervousness. After all, the class might be awesome, and by the end of class – even if it isn't awesome – it's likely your fear and nervousness will have completely disappeared anyway. You also now know not to come back to that studio.

3. Find an ally

When we're afraid or nervous our attention is mostly focussed on our own experience. We're freaking out too much to notice anything else. Challenge yourself to get out of your experience and notice what's going on around you.

Take a few deep breaths and check out the other people coming into the studio or class. Do any of them look brand new? Is anyone else filling in the registration form? Do any of them look as nervous as you feel? If someone does and the opportunity arises or you're bold enough to take the opportunity, reach out to that person and connect with them.

A simple, 'Your first time too huh?' is enough to convey important information. That you're both newbies, and that you're open and interested in them. Whether or not they take up your opening is irrelevant – just reaching out is sometimes enough to reduce our own fear or intimidation.

4. Remember everyone was once a newbie

Even if you don't have a friend, the studio or teacher wasn't very welcoming and there are no other new students there... you can still help to calm your fear and nerves by remembering this.

Every single person in the room was once brand new to yoga.

They were all newbies once upon a time. Most of them would have started class with no idea of the difference between Shalabasana and Shavasana. Many of them wouldn't have been able to touch their toes, or stand on one leg, or chant om without giggling out loud.

Even your teacher would have been a newbie once. Sure, they look super confident, bendy and strong now... but once upon a time, they were just like you. In fact, they're probably just like you more than you realise.

5. It's okay, you're okay

Finally, remember that it's okay to be as scared or nervous as you are.

You're not trying to deny your fear or get rid of it here, I just want you to realise that everybody has it and it's all okay.

Feeling fear or feeling nervousness won't kill you. It's just an emotion, and like all emotions, they come, they go, they peak, they trough, they fade away, they rise up again.

Emotions mean you're alive and you're a human being and both of those things are miracles of life. So feel that fear, feel that nervousness and rock the class anyway. Not by being amazing at the postures, but simply by being there. Right there, with your emotions, as they are.

Now that is yoga.

Coming home: the ultimate teacher is you a.k.a don't give your power away!

As a beginning student – hell, even as a long-time yoga student – this concept can be difficult to grasp.

The ultimate teacher is you.

Yes, you are your own authority. You know what's best for you.

'Hang on a second – I haven't even started yoga, I don't know anything about postures and you're telling me I am my own best teacher?'

Ultimately – yes. At first, though, you are going to have to rely on the teaching and guidance of other more knowledgeable yoga students. I specifically call your yoga teachers *students* to remind you that we're all learning, all of the time. Some of us have spent longer immersed in yoga than others, so have more knowledge of the terrain and understanding of the world, but we're still a student, just like you are.

We're going to get it wrong sometimes, we will make mistakes and we don't always know what's best for you.

That's why it's important – even as a beginning student to re-member that ultimately you are your own teacher.

Let's get clear on which you we're talking about. Remember we spoke about the idea of the small you – ego identity – and the big You? It's the big You that is your ultimate teacher. When you first start yoga, it's likely that you haven't yet connected to that big You, or the small you is so loud you can barely hear the voice of the big You.

It's the small you that insists on doing full Chaturanga Dandasana (Plank Pose) even though your body would be much better served by keeping the knees on the ground for extra support. It's the small you that refuses to take Child's Pose even when the arms are burning and the breath is ragged. It's the small you that gets right into going to class... and then just stops one day without realising why. In each of these circumstances the choice that you made was based on what you wanted – attachment – or what you didn't want – aversion. It was never about what you *needed*.

You may want to do full Chaturanga Dandasana because you've got an image of yourself as strong and capable, and putting your knees down would contradict that image of you. Or because you're afraid that people would think you were weak or less than or be-cause you're used to pushing through pain.

A wise teacher will see all of this at play and gently guide you toward the correct variation for your body and your current needs.

In time, as you connect more and more with the deeper sense of Self – with You, you'll be able to make that choice yourself. You won't need a teacher to guide you toward what you need, rather than what you want. You'll feel the correctness of that choice within you.

Making this shift from identifying mostly with the small you with its wants, attachments and aversions to identifying mostly with the big You with its clarity around what is needed in any given moment *is* Yoga. That's what it's all about. This is you coming home to You. It's union right there baby!

On a practical level, it's useful to be aware of this shift because it can help keep you on track and safe in class. Not every teacher you work with is wise and not every teacher will know what you need in any given moment. The more you learn to connect with that deeper sense of Self, the more you can guide yourself through class appropriately. At times, your internal guidance may even contradict what the teacher is instructing you to do and you have to have faith that you know best for yourself.

I've been in a yoga class with an excellent teacher who didn't realise that my sciatic pain was playing up sending shooting pain down my right leg. Every time we went into a standing forward bend, I would bend my knees because I could feel that felt better and safe for me. I didn't know at the time it's crucial to do this in standing forward bends when you're experiencing sciatica. My internal teacher was taking good care of me, and because I'd long ago learned to trust my instincts, I went with it.

A few times, the teacher walked up and asked me to straighten my legs – she knew I had the flexibility to do so. If I'd been a beginning student, I wouldn't have necessarily known enough to trust my instincts. I may have straightened my legs, which would have put more strain on my spine and discs. But when she made that request, I checked in with my Self and it felt like staying bent was the way to be. So I stayed bent.

Mostly though, when we first start going to class, we don't know anything and it's our small self getting in the way. That's why learning to surrender to the teacher is part of the process – assuming they are a good teacher and we can trust them! We have to believe that they have our best interests at heart and can see what we need to do.

Within this surrender though, even as a total beginner, always keep your bullshit detector turned on and if anything feels wrong to you and you feel yourself wanting to resist or stop or check out – take a moment. Breathe into wherever you are and ask the deeper part of you, 'What's going on? What do I need to do right now?'

This is especially important if you have any kind of injury or illness that's affecting your body. Yes, you need to trust and work with your teacher, but you also need to retain autonomy and never be afraid to question what the teacher is telling you. Maybe you don't question it in the middle of class, perhaps you wait until after class, but ask those questions.

Understand too that the ego is wily – it will do anything it can to keep you locked behind old defences and stuck in old behaviour patterns. Much of what comes up in class – the resistance, the desire to stop or check out or leave – that's the ego kicking back and trying hard to retain control. So there is a fine line to walk and it's natural to fall over many times. Over time, you learn discernment, and you can tell when your reaction in class is all about ego, or all about what you really need.

This discernment is yoga – knowing what the truth is, what the reality is, and what action to take. This is why consistent practice of Yoga brings us home to our ultimate teacher – our Self.

6. IN CLASS

Why is the breath so important in yoga?

By now, you'll have realised that Yoga is about more than just postures. Yet postures are still a powerful way to practice yoga. However, take a moment to consider what the difference is between say yoga postures and gymnastics.

Many of the body shapes are similar or exactly the same in both pursuits – think of the splits in gymnastics, known as Hanumanasana in yoga or performing a backbend in gymnastics, known as Urdhva Dhanurasana in Yoga. Same shape yet two very different experiences. One is simply moving the body in a particular way, the other is a path to liberation.

What defines that difference?

It's the breath – or rather awareness of breath. In both instances, the gymnast and the yogi will be breathing. But in one, the gymnast isn't necessarily aware of his breath. The yogi is bringing full awareness to her breath. Even if the gymnast is aware of his breath, he won't be actively working with it in the way the yogi will be. A yogi maintains awareness of breath as a tool for becoming aware of the relationship they are having with the posture. When a yogi comes into a posture, fully aware of the breath, she will use that awareness of breath to consciously bring awareness into the parts of the body that feel tense and stuck, breathing into those areas. With dedicated practice over time, a yogi doesn't just breathe into her lungs, she can breathe right into her hips or spine or even feet.

How is this possible? We'll come back to that question, but first, let's take a moment to consider our breath.

Breath is the one function in the body that is both unconscious and conscious. Every single day, you take about 25,000 breaths and most of those are unconscious. When you practice yoga, you start to become conscious of your breath.

This is the first important thing to notice – the breath acts as a bridge between the unconscious and the conscious.

First, we're unconsciously breathing. Then, we become conscious of our breathing. To do this we have to focus our awareness, so now we've become aware. The unconscious has become conscious via the bridge of the breath.

It is at this point, with awareness of breath, that you may notice you hold your breath slightly on the inhale or that your breath sounds ragged, like the edges of a saw or that you only feel like you're breathing into one side of your lungs. All of this information is important – it points to aspects of yourself that you were unconscious of before.

Armed with this information, you can allow yourself to let go of that holding on the inhale and notice how it affects your postures. You may notice how it affects your psyche.

Let's do some breath work right now.

- Place both hands lightly on your belly. Exhale all the air out your lungs through your nose.
- Now inhale (through the nose) slow and strong right down into your belly, allowing your hands to expand slowly outward.
- Exhale again, all of that air.
- Inhale thoroughly.
- Keep moving your hands with your breath, up and down, up and down.

Listen to the sound of your breath. Notice its rhythm. Pay attention to how smooth it is, whether the inhale and the exhale are the same length, and if the breath gets caught or is ragged in any way. Get up close and intimate with your breath, curious about how it behaves.

Now you're breathing – this is abdominal breathing. It's the first way beginning yoga students are taught to breathe.

As you read through this article, keep breathing down into your belly and see if you can remain aware of both the words you're reading and the breath in your body.

This is difficult to do. Most of us aren't used to breathing with awareness – we've never needed to do so. Staying focused on our breathing while also paying attention to what we're doing seems downright impossible – yet this is what we're asked to do in yoga class. We're asked to come into strange shapes with our bodies while retaining breath awareness. Often, we're told exactly when to inhale and when to exhale.

This takes practice – hence the term, yoga practice.

As well as being entirely unaware of our breathing, most of us aren't breathing properly either. Our breath is constricted or tight and often we spend all day shallow breathing – just breathing into the upper lobes of the lungs. That means that only a small amount of air is taken in and the oxygen contained in that air has to nourish every single cell in your body.

However, breathe properly using your full lung capacity and you send oxygen flooding into every single cell in your body. Yep – your cells breathe. The air doesn't just come into your lungs, it's taken to every single cell in your body via your circulation system. Every cell in your body inhales the oxygen and exhales the carbon dioxide – a process called respiration.

Breathing is important because our cells constantly need a new supply of oxygen so they can produce energy – without this vital oxygen, cellular function is impaired, and damage or cell death is possible.

After all, you can live for weeks without food or days without water. How long can you without air? Maybe six minutes?

Air is the very essence of life.

That is why in Vedic and Yogic tradition, air is linked to prana – the life force that flows through all living creatures – plant and animal. This is why working with the breath is called pranayama – often translated as breath exercises. However, while pranayama does involve different ways to breathe, the real reason we're manipulating the breath like this is to play with prana. It's not about the breath as such.

Yet breath and prana are intimately intertwined – breathing is the major way we bring more prana into our bodies and using our breath we can manipulate the flow of prana around the nadis or channels in our bodies. (See the chapter on *'Kundalini, prana, nadis, chakras and the subtle body'*.)

In Sanskrit the word prana breaks down like this. The root word 'pra,' meaning 'to fill,' is added to the root word, 'an,' ('to breathe' or 'to live') creating the new meaning 'the life that fills with the breath.' In other words, prana is the life principle in action.

Prana is commonly translated as 'air,' 'breath,' 'spirit,' 'life,' 'life force,' 'energy,' or 'subtle energy.'

So prana literally means 'breathing forth' the universal life force.

In my role as a yoga teacher, I notice how people breathe. I watch people stand up to make a speech at a wedding or the like, and I can tell from their breathing how the experience is for them.

Someone who is nervous and fearful may get up and take short, sharp breaths, or they may hold their breath very tight. Perhaps they barely breathe at all. If this is happening and the speechmaker is aware of yoga, breath and prana, all they have to do is bring attention to their breath and allow themselves to breathe slowly and fully. This helps to ground them and calm their nervous system. Suddenly, they're able to speak far better than they were before – all because they altered their breathing pattern.

Remember, breathing is an automatic function and it's controlled by the autonomic nervous system. But our nervous system has two parts: the sympathetic and the parasympathetic nervous systems.

The sympathetic is the fight or flight system – it prepares the body for sudden stress by controlling physical things like our heart rate, the adrenal glands and our breathing. The parasympathetic system does the opposite – it prepares the body for rest, and also helps the digestive system work more efficiently to extract nutrients from our food.

When you are in a fearful situation, this means the sympathetic nervous system has been triggered, but you can consciously shift the body back into the parasympathetic system using your breath. This is part of conscious living – paying attention to the physicality of your body, the heart rate, the sweat glands, the breath, the adrenal glands and consciously shifting it via breathing. It's a simple technique and it's very powerful. It all comes back to awareness and breath.

If you spend your entire day breathing shallow, short, sharp breaths, you are likely keeping your body in the sympathetic system, and this signals stress to the body. It's no wonder so many people feel stressed out – their breathing makes their body react as if they are; so they are.

This is why proper breathing is the heart of both yoga and meditation – without breath, you don't have a yoga posture. Conscious awareness of breath is the first step in waking up and becoming more conscious in every aspect of your life. When you notice your breath it gives you information about how you're relating to each moment.

As you increase the amount of oxygen in your body, your pranic body starts to come alive. Plus, the coordination of your inhalation and exhalation with the movements of your physical body, as in Sun Salutations, is one of the ways in which the physical body and breath body become synchronized with the mental body (concentration and awareness).

Breathing is the most vital action we take in our lives, because it is the essence of life for us. Yet it is also the most unconscious action that we take. For this reason, becoming conscious of how you breathe and then deliberately directing the flow of breath and prana into your body is the single most powerful action you can take toward living a conscious life.

The reason you feel so amazing after a yoga class is not about the postures and the stretching and the moving. It's because you just spent ninety minutes paying attention to your breathing. It's because you have flooded every cell in your body with an abundance of oxygen and those cells are firing with energy. It's because you have consciously connected to prana – the life force that permeates the universe.

Whatever it is that ails you – whether it's an agitated mind, a dullness of body, an addiction to food or an inability to express emotions – simply starting to breathe properly can have a profound effect on your experience of life.

Take a deep breath now and ride that wave into your body.

Follow it, feel it, experience it.

Your breath is the bridge between mind, body and soul.

Connect with your breath and you connect with who you truly are. You don't have to be in yoga class to take advantage of this – it's the kind of practice you can easily bring into your everyday life. Every time you feel stressed – bring awareness to your breathing. Every time you feel upset, afraid or emotional, bring awareness to your breath. When you feel tired, anxious or nervous – bring awareness to your breathing.

Allow yourself to take a deep, full breath. Let that breath naturally lengthen and open the body. Feel how it calms your mind. Feel how it brings you into the present. This is why the breath is so important in yoga – it is yoga.

How to approach asana & alignment

It's easy before we start yoga, even when we are practicing yoga and going to class, to have this idea that the aim is to bend our bodies into this perfect posture. However, this is not true at all – this is mistaking the map for the terrain as such.

Remember, the aim of yoga is to be present with what is, which is self-realisation. The reason we practice postures is that it helps us to be present with the moment – even if that is a posture that doesn't look anything like the cover of *Yoga Journal*.

Plus we practice postures because in becoming present with what is, we start to shift our identification with our thoughts, our feelings and even our body. This is the process of self-realisation – realising that the Self is none of these things – that we are not our thoughts, not our feelings and not even our bodies.

Therefore, doing a pose 'right' is nothing to do with the posture *looking* a certain way. If it was, gymnasts and contortionists would be the most amazing yogis in the world, because they can do all kinds of fancy and advanced postures 'right'. However, just because they're bending their body into a particular shape, it doesn't mean that they're practicing yoga. It doesn't mean that they are completely in the present moment, aware of their breath and it doesn't mean that they are observing their thoughts and feelings and starting to shift from identifying with those thoughts and feelings to identifying with that which *witnesses* the thoughts and feelings.

Doing a pose 'right' can happen even when you're not super bendy. Doing Downward Dog right doesn't necessarily mean straight legs and heels on the ground. If your hamstrings are tight, you may not be able to straighten your legs without compromising the alignment of your spine or pelvis. You may need to keep your knees bent to allow the pelvis to tilt forward and free the spine. Creating the right alignment in the spine means that your breath is free and open too – and that's where Adho Mukha Svanasana really starts. In fact, that's where most asana starts – with awareness of breath and by extension, awareness of prana.

A straight spine and aligned pelvis means that your breath has a clear line to move along and this is important because it creates a free flow of energy up the spine, which is a big thing in yoga.

It doesn't matter if you're in Garudasana (Eagle Pose), Navasana (Boat Pose), Ardha Chandrasana (Half Moon Pose) or Gomukhasana (Cow Pose), finding your breath in your spine is what helps to open into the posture.

Even in asana where the spine is bending, it's still important to find your breath so that the spine remains open, even while bending.

Imagine your spine is a garden hose. Bend that hose into a C-shape that keeps the air flowing through the hose. That's an open spine. Now bend the garden hose so it cuts off the flow of air through it. That's a closed spine.

In your first few classes or for the first few years – it really helps if you're aware that doing the pose 'right' isn't about looking like the teacher, or *Yoga Journal*. It's about finding the openness of breath within the current limitations of your body.

A good teacher will be able to guide you into asana variations that allow you to support your body wherever it is. Things like bent legs, or sitting on a block in seated asana or sometimes even using a wall to support yourself in asana like Garudasana or Ardha Chandrasana.

Now back to prana. This awareness of the flow of breath isn't just about oxygen. It's about the flow of prana around the body...

something your teacher may or may not mention, but it's happening nonetheless.

In fact, Shakti is the essence of Hatha Yoga – Shakti being an expression of prana within our bodies, just like a river is an expression of water moving through the land. Remember Hatha Yoga is the yoga of physical postures, as opposed to say Karma Yoga which is the yoga of our actions within the world.

I've talked about prana in the chapter on *'Kundalini, prana, nadis, chakras and the subtle body'*.

A brief recap – prana is the Sanskrit word for life force, and it permeates everything in the entire universe. Prana derives from the Sankrit word "pra" meaning "to fill", added to the root word "an" which means "to breathe" or "to live".

In the human body, prana is like an electrical force and it travels around on channels (like wires) called nadis. Some nadis are big and thick like a state highway, some small and skinny like a country road.

When the body is all tight and weak, it's like those nadis have landslides blocking them or they're all cracked and weak. Prana can't travel freely, so you're not getting energy to all your body's cells.

As you get stronger and more open, the nadis open up and more and more prana can flow freely along them. Your entire body becomes energised – which is one reason why yoga makes you feel so good.

So when you practice asana, it is about finding the alignment of the muscles, bones and organs which creates shapes that look a certain way.

Yet another way to think about it is rearranging your physical body around energetic lines so prana can flow freely.

This is the inside-out method of asana, as opposed to the outside-in method; both of which end up in the same place.

Therefore doing asana 'right' isn't so much about being perfect in the pose, but being perfect with where you are at in the pose – bent legs and all; so that prana can flow freely – starting with the pelvis and spine usually and then moving out into the limbs.

At first when you practice, you may not be able to tune into the subtle sensation of prana in the body – but you can tune into the feeling of breath in your body.

Make your focus finding your breath first in the nostrils, then in the lungs and finally out into the spine, limbs and extremities; eventually you'll begin to discern prana flowing around your body.

In class, how does this translate?

It means that when you're thinking about alignment, you need to pay attention to what your limitations are and understand how to work with them. Most beginners need to do all forward bends with at the very least a micro-bend in the knees, sometimes with a deeper bend in the knees. This helps the pelvis to hinge forward and helps to release the spine. Otherwise, bending forward will actually pull the pelvis backwards and you end up with a rounded spine.

This doesn't allow for free-flowing prana and it's not great for the body either.

Ideally, when you first start yoga, you'll have a great teacher who will be able to help you learn about your body and what you need to do to modify the postures to make them safe and useful for you. Your responsibility is to let go of the idea that you're attempting to attain a *Yoga Journal* idea of perfection and instead be okay with being where you are – modifications and all.

As a teacher, I can see where students need to be and I can also see those students who resist my cues and modifications because they want to look a certain way or they don't want to acknowledge the reality of their bodies.

These are the students who don't yet have an open and moving pelvis, yet refuse to bend their legs in Downward Dog or the students who haven't yet built up the strength and body aware-ness to hold Chaturanga Dandasana without sagging through the midsection.

No matter how many times I cue students to bring their knees down until they build up their strength, they refuse. Time after time, they go into Chaturanga and they sag, putting stress on their joints and likely doing their body harm. It's difficult to build up the correct strength and body awareness from this position.

It's all about pride, attachment and desire – the very things we come to yoga to learn all about. Those students who are able to let go of their pride, and their attachment to doing the full posture or their desire to achieve or progress in class may have postures that look less advanced, but in reality, their practice is far more advanced than the students doing more 'advanced postures' with pride, attachment and desire.

It's okay to start yoga with modifications. It's okay to use props. It's okay to bend your knees. It's okay to lean against the wall.

Give yourself permission to be easy and gentle on yourself when you first start. Meet yourself right where you are. If this is difficult – inquire into that difficulty. Why do you resist putting your knees on the floor when your body sags? What are you afraid of? What are you attached to? What do you desire?

This is the work of Yoga – this is what you are here for.

Yoga injuries: how to keep yourself safe

Ultimately, it's your responsibility to look after yourself in class, even though when we first start we usually think that the teacher is going to be doing that for us. A good teacher will create a safe learning environment, but even a good teacher doesn't know your body as well as you know your own body. Keep responsibility for your own body and allow your teacher to guide you. That way, if you've both got safety in mind, you're far less likely to injure yourself in yoga.

Because people do – all the time; people injure themselves because of the way they're doing the yoga, not because there's anything wrong with the yoga itself.

Here are the steps you can take to make sure you don't injure yourself in class.

1. *Make sure you inform the teacher of any injury or medical condition that may impact your ability to move*

This includes prior operations that affect movement such as spinal fusions, knee operations, and shoulder operations. If you've recently had surgery and are still healing, it's also wise to inform the teacher – you don't want to stretch the stitched area and pop a stitch or two.

You also need to inform the teacher if you have chronic conditions that could impact on class – like diabetes, high blood pressure or epilepsy. If you have a heart condition, or have had a heart attack or stroke – tell the teacher. In fact, it's better to err on the side of caution when it comes to disclosure. Why? Because yoga postures are powerful things and some are contraindicated for some conditions. That means if you've got detached retinas, you don't want to practice headstand. If you're pregnant or even think you're pregnant, yoga in the first trimester is usually advised against unless you've already got a regular practice.

A good teacher will collect this kind of information from you before class, usually in a registration form so they have it on file. However, sometimes there is no registration, and no opportunity to even speak to the teacher before class.

That's why it's so important that you show up early before your first class with any new teacher. At least fifteen minutes early is good, but 20 to 25 minutes is better. Teachers can be busy before class and you want to have a quiet moment to connect with them.

Don't let your own shyness or fear of speaking up get in the way either. You have to take care of yourself and if the teacher doesn't know you just had an operation on your knee a few months ago they may wrongly push you further in some postures than you need to go.

2. During class, if the instructions for a posture aren't clear and it's a difficult and potentially dangerous posture, don't be afraid to speak up, or opt out and take Child's Pose

If the teacher questions you, that's when you can say – 'I haven't done this posture before and the instructions weren't clear'. I've been in class where teachers say, 'Alright, and now take yourself into headstand'. There's no alignment instruction at all. Yes, the teacher may walk around and assist people, but a posture like headstand takes patience and time to build toward. There are elements of openness and strength that need to be attained before headstand is attempted; otherwise it's possible to damage the neck.

If you don't know the posture, and you don't understand the cues – opt out or speak up.

3. Don't be afraid to opt out of something that you know it's bad for you

I used to keep a bend in my knees in all standing forward bends, and seated forward bends because I had a tendency toward herniated discs in my spine. Keeping that bend allowed my pelvis more freedom of movement and kept my spine from rounding.

I've been in classes where teachers encourage me to straighten my legs because that's how the posture is done properly or because they think they're helping me go further. I know I need to keep my legs bent. Yet even after a decade of practicing and teaching, I find it hard to stick to what I know works for me when the teacher is saying something different. I want to do what the teacher says – it's the natural inclination, to please or seek approval.

When you first start yoga, it's almost impossible to do something different from the teacher's instruction, because we think the teacher knows best. Sometimes, they do. But it's our body and if we get injured, we're the ones that suffer. So err on the side of caution and listen to what your body is telling you.

4. After class, get the teacher to explain any posture that felt wrong or painful to you

A good teacher will take the time to instruct you into the posture and help you find correct alignment for your body. If you are doing this, pay strong attention to the feedback and instruction you're given and when you get home, practice! That way, by the time you get to class next week, you'll remember what the teacher said and you don't have to ask them again to explain after class. There's a fine line between being a responsible student and being an annoying student.

5. Check your ego at the door. Yoga is not a competition.

Often it's not poor instruction from the teacher that injures us, but our interpretation of the teacher's instruction. As beginning students we want to do a good job, we want to keep up and we want to impress people. Even if we don't realise this aspect of ourselves at play... it is! This means we can often push ourselves too hard too fast.

During class, I can see students who need to back off and take it easy, and I will always cue options in the sequence that allow people to work at their own pace. I will invite students to rest in Child's Pose or stay in Downward Dog. Yet so often, I'll watch students who would benefit most from resting in Child's Pose struggling to hold Downward Dog and losing all form and awareness because they're too stressed and their body is going into fight or flight mode.

A great teacher will keep bringing you back to where you need to be, but in a class with an average teacher, you're left to flail on your own. If you don't take responsibility for your own well-being, you could repeatedly push yourself through every class and end up injuring yourself because fatigue means you're not able to stay in proper alignment.

6. *Always stay connected to your breath*

This is the number one way to make sure you don't injure yourself – let your breath led you into postures as it will never take you wrong.

Once, I was getting an intense adjustment from a teacher in an Ashtanga class. I was in a seated twist and I stopped breathing and subtly resisted the very posture I was meant to be opening up into. That resistance and lack of breath meant my body seized up and I aggravated my sciatic pain. After weeks of practice of that same posture I finally clued in to what I was doing, and with patience and awareness I was able to teach myself to breathe into the posture, and the pain subsided.

If you've stopped breathing, you're resisting the posture and that's when you'll injure yourself. If you're not aware of your breath, you're likely not aware of your body either, and that's another key time where you may injure yourself.

Stay connected to your breath, listen to your body, know your limitations and don't be afraid to opt out or ask for clearer instructions. It's your body – take care of it!

Adjustments: yes or no?

A yoga class can be a hands-on touchy-feely kind of place. Yoga teachers are generally very comfortable with both their own bodies and the bodies of other people. We're always looking to see how you're lining things up and what parts you're activating and where you need to shift things slightly and where you're holding tension.

Often, as well as giving verbal cues for alignment, we'll use physical cues as well – although not all styles of yoga or all teachers do this. These cues are called 'adjustments'. Adjustments come in a wide variety of forms, which depends largely on the style of yoga and the teacher administering the adjustments.

Some forms like Ashtanga use what can be aggressive adjustments – it can feel like a teacher is wrenching the student into position. In the hands of a skilled and experienced teacher, this kind of adjustment can help a student break through a long-held movement pattern and activate new sensations in the body – 'Oh! That's where I'm meant to be in this posture!' The muscles feel it, the nerves feel it, and after that, the student can sometimes easily get back into the adjusted position without the help of the teacher.

In more general classes, especially with beginners, a teacher might use a more gentle form of adjustment – usually not taking a student deeper into the posture, but correcting a misalignment, like straightening up an arm or shifting a drooping inner knee.

A more rare form of adjustment is energetic alignment. This is one way I was taught to adjust students. Instead of moving them toward something, you use a hand or stand where you want the student to move toward – you give them something to aim for. They move themselves, based on where you are. An example of this is placing a hand on the outside of the front bent knee in Warrior II and asking the student to press into your hand. They activate their inner thigh and find the correct knee alignment by following your instruction.

Finally, a common adjustment in many classes is given in Child's Pose. Child's Pose reveals what's going on in our hips, knees, ankles, spines and shoulders – almost the whole body! A good teacher can tell where a student is holding tension and gently press into that area – whether it's pushing the hips further down onto the heels or lengthening the spine out and away from the pelvis.

Like anything in yoga, adjustments can be dangerous. A yoga teacher might be inexperienced, not pay close enough attention to the student's actual experience or not know the student's body well enough. If you've got an old injury or weakness in the body and a teacher attempts to strongly adjust you into the 'right position', they can hurt you.

If you're 100% healthy and don't mind being adjusted, you don't really need to do or say anything. But if you *don't* want to be adjusted and you're in a new class, you need to let the teacher know – especially if you notice that they seem to be the adjusting kind. (Some teachers always adjust, some never adjust, most fall somewhere in between.)

A simple, "I don't like being adjusted," or, "Please, no adjustments" will suffice. You don't have to say why – no explanation is necessary. A good teacher will accept your boundary at face value. If, over time, you develop a relationship with that teacher, you may change your mind about being adjusted. Or, the teacher may gently ask if this kind of adjustment is okay.

Staying present in class, and aware of the teacher, is also an important way to maintain boundaries around adjustment. A good teacher will usually pause beside a student and take a moment to psychically step into the student's space before doing an adjustment.

Usually the teacher is watching your breath pattern and also synchronising their breath with yours so they can more accurately feel what you're experiencing. That's the moment where you can shake your head, or say, 'no thanks' quietly. A good teacher will hear both your non-verbal and verbal cues and move on.

If you do get adjusted when you don't want to be, take a moment after class to let the teacher know you don't want adjustments

– you don't have to say why. Remember, it's your body and your yoga experience. You don't have to conform to anyone else's expectations.

On the flip side of that – some students absolutely love getting adjustments because adjustments can help us progress our practice and release tension we can't otherwise access. One major reason why I choose to study with my current teacher, Peter Sanson, is that he is highly experienced and gives amazing adjustments. His hands-on work with my practice has taken it to places I never thought I'd be. So it's worth seeking out teachers who are skilled at adjustments – they can be incredible to work with.

I still remember my first Bikram Yoga teacher – Tanya Harrington – who gave the most delicious adjustments in face-down Shavasana during the spine-strengthening series. Bikram teachers aren't taught to adjust students and they're not supposed to, but Tanya knew exactly what she was doing. She'd stand gently on my up-turned feet in Shavasana and walk her feet up and down, giving a foot to foot massage that released any spinal tension that might have been accumulating through the postures. I'd always pray that she'd pick me to adjust during class!

You won't always come across such skilled and compassionate teachers though, so even if you love adjustments, always remember it's your body and you're responsible for taking care of it. Stay attuned to the quality of adjustments you receive from your teachers and let them know if they're doing anything that's hurting or even just not quite right.

Don't ever give your power or authority away. Yes, they are the teacher, but it's your body. Remember that.

What does it mean to "breathe into it"?

There are loads of phrases which yoga teachers toss around willy nilly that after a time cease to have any real meaning.
Phrases like:

- Surrender into the pose
- Let your heart open
- Find your centre
- Honour yourself
- Let yourself come into a place of...
- Honour yourself for committing to your practice today...

I know, I say these things. Thing is, many of these phrases have value and depth, and – in the right circumstances – apply to the practice.

In particular, the much over-used "breathe into it" is gold – when you know what it means and how to apply it.

The problem is, many people in a yoga class have no idea how to breathe into anything other than their lungs and many even struggle with that.

So what does "breathe into it mean"?

First, a detour.

Yoga as a practice is best taught one on one with a teacher who can respond to the actual needs of the student as they arise. That means that if and when the phrase "breathe into it" was used, the student would both need to hear that particular phrase and be ready to grasp and apply what it means.

However, 99% of us learn yoga in class situations, where the teacher is speaking to anywhere from five students to 100 students all at different places and stages in their understanding of yoga. The phrase "breathe into it" might be perfect for one student in the room at one time, and completely useless for all the rest.

Until the day when it does become useful and you suddenly get it and realise, oh... *that's* what that teacher's been going on about for all this time.

That's it indeed.

So if you don't know how to "breathe into it" in your yoga, don't worry about it. It doesn't matter, with practice, attention and intention, one day you will know.

That said, it doesn't hurt to also apply yourself by reading and practicing at home, playing with the concept of 'breathing into it' all by yourself. That's a great way to learn yoga.

Now. When I practice yoga, I breathe into it all the time. In fact, breathing into my body is how I practice.

It is first and foremost the only action that initiates and drives everything else. From a place of stillness, I breathe. That breath travels – or experientially appears to travel – all around my body. That breath then moves my body according to what asana I'm currently practicing or about to practice.

In Tadasana (Mountain Pose) this means that from a standing tall position, I breathe down into my lungs, allowing my rib cage to expand and drop. The breath travels down my spine into my pelvis and lengthens my tailbone to the ground. As I inhale, the breath travels back up my spine and lengthens the crown of my head towards the sky.

On the next exhale, I again feel the breath dropping down through the body, down the back of the body and into the heels and my feet release into the earth – in essence, grounding. The inhale again rises up the body and my sternum may lift and my collarbones broaden.

Every inhale expands and opens my body according to where I'm holding tension and what the potential of the posture is.

Every exhale grounds and deepens the posture, according to what parts of the body are touching the ground and where I need to soften.

This is what "breathing into it" means – it's an organic and internal process that allows the yoga posture to open up from within. Every movement, every posture, all the time. That's yoga.

Now, if you're just beginning yoga, you've got no idea how to breathe into your spine, let alone your feet.

How on earth to you get from where you are now to where I am now?

Practice. Intention. Imagination. Openness. Willingness.

That's how.

The first step in learning how to let your breath lead your yoga is to simply be aware of your breath as it is, in every moment.

At this stage, you're not trying to change anything, fix anything or direct anything. You're just noticing what is. You'll notice where you hold your breath and where you take short sharp breaths and where your breath gets stuck. That's your breath talking to you and giving you feedback about how you're experiencing the posture. Notice it. Learn to respond to it.

Case in point.

I'm at Bikram Yoga. We're going into a standing backbend. The woman beside me is taking short gasping breaths, as if she's a goldfish that's been tossed from her bowl. Her breath is telling her all kinds of things right now – but unless she knows to listen to it, she likely hasn't even noticed what's going on.

She's got no idea what her breath is telling her, and I know that because she's not responding to the messages.

So before you even think about breathing into anything, you need to learn to listen.

Which brings me back to my initial point about over-used phrases in yoga classes. They sound empty and meaningless much of the time – because they are unless they are specifically directed at a student who needs to hear that actual phrase in that precise moment. Otherwise, they're just catch-all sound-good yoga-speak.

But when they are directed at a student – especially one who hears the phrase and is able to respond to it – the energy in the room knows. There's a collective noticing of the specific directive and the specific response.

So next time you hear a phrase in class and you have no idea what it means, take the time to go and ask the teacher afterwards. If they're a decent yoga teacher, they'll be able to tell you what it means and how it applies to your practice. If they're really good, they may even be able to demonstrate what it means.

If you came up to me at the end of class and asked me what it means to breathe into it, here's what I'd say to you; or rather what I'd get you to experience.

Camel Pose is one of my most favourite postures for demonstrating the need to breathe into anything. So often people assume the starting position, physically crank themselves back into the backbend and *then* attempt to breathe.

Instead, my suggestion is to assume a starting position – kneeling straight up with the hands on the hips, fingers facing up.

Next comes the breath – before moving, before bending back, before going anywhere. This is where we get to practice *breathing into it*.

As you exhale, extend your tailbone towards the ground creating space in your lower spine and squeeze your inner thighs together.

As you inhale, press your hips forward and allow the breath to rise up the front of the body lifting the sternum toward the sky.

At this point, the head may or may not begin to look up and back.

Repeat – exhale and find stability, strength and grounding. Inhale and find expansion, lift and opening.

Oscillating between the inhale and exhale like this – rooting and growing – you'll find that Camel naturally opens up. You don't have to move your body anywhere – you are moved into it. Best of all, you are moved into it with a full, natural, expansive breath.

That's breathing into it.

We notice where we're holding tension in a posture. We bring attention to our breath. We allow our breath to be soft and full, maintaining that dual attention on breathing and the place of tension. That willful connection of the two concepts in our mind is enough. Breath enters the area of tension. Tension melts.

Next time you're in a yoga class and the teacher says either to the class or to you in particular, "breathe into it", here's how to respond.

Check and see it applies to you – start by listening to your breath. Is it soft and full? If it's tight or you're holding the breath, back out of the posture until you reach a place where you can breathe comfortably and allow the breath to take you back into the posture.

Check in on your body – are you subconsciously resisting the posture in any way? Can you sense any tension in your body? Keep your attention on that place in the body and bring full attention to your breath as well. Focus on letting go on the exhale, softening and releasing as much as you can. Keep that dual awareness going.

Finally, maintain that awareness on your breath and surrender to its directive – let your breath take you into the postures, oscillating inhale and exhale by oscillating inhale and exhale. That's it, now you know what it means to 'breathe into it'. Now you can make it work for you.

Strangeness on the mat: crying, laughing, groaning, farting, grimaces & twitches

The first time I remember crying in a yoga class was back in about 2000. I was living in Whistler and going to class at the recently opened Neo-Alpine Bikram Studio. We came into Standing Bow Posture – always a struggle for me with tight hips and a dodgy lower back. I started sobbing. Deep, wrenching sobs from the pit of my belly. My yoga teacher – one of the best Bikram Teachers that I've ever had, Tanya Harrington – gently guided me down into Child's Pose and just told me to stay there until I felt ready to continue the rest of the class.

We're not always this fortunate the first time we hit strangeness on the yoga mat. Often, we have no idea what's happening to us and the yoga teacher doesn't either. Like me, you might find yourself sobbing, weeping or crying softly. You might be unable to suppress out-of-place laughter. You might find yourself groaning, growling, hacking or making all kinds of strange guttural noises.

But it's not just noises that create strangeness on the yoga mat. Our body can also do strange out-of-control things. Our lip might do an Elvis-curl as we attempt Kundalini-style arm rotations. Or our eyes might roll back in our head during Breath of Fire Pranayama. Sometimes our body can twitch and jerk uncontrollably, especially in Shavasana.

The good news is – all of this is normal. In fact, with regular yoga practice, all of this can be *expected* in some way shape or form.

As we learned in earlier chapters, yoga is about far more than physical postures and affects more than our muscles and ligaments. When we practice yoga, we're affecting our nervous system, and we're also releasing blockages of all kinds that may have been in our bodies for decades. On a practical level, that can mean old, unexpressed emotions rising to the surface, and sometimes old memories too.

As a child, I completely shut down emotionally and didn't cry for about two decades. By the time I hit the yoga mat in my late twenties, there were oceans of tears waiting to be expressed. After that first Bikram class back in 2000, I cried my way through Bikram classes in Whistler, Canada, and then in Dunedin, Queenstown, Wellington and Napier New Zealand. It's now 2014 and I still haven't hit the bottom of that well, although I think I can see it.

So rest assured, weeping in yoga class is normal.

The question is, what to do about it? If you're having some kind of strange experience on the yoga mat, the first port of call is to touch base with your yoga teacher. Hopefully you've got a skilful, experienced, intuitive and respectful teacher. Sometimes just asking a question can help us feel more comfortable. 'When we come into pigeon pose, I just want to cry.' A good teacher will be able to reassure you, and perhaps give you some instruction on how you may want to approach a particular posture.

While emotional releases need to be approached with kindness, compassion and patience, there's often not much we can do about strange happenings in our nervous system.

Our lips might curl, our eyes might roll, our tongue might curve back into our mouth... these things just happen.

Know that it's normal and it's okay. If it does make you feel uncomfortable, it can help to position yourself in the class where you feel inconspicuous. You can always ask the teacher – those who have at least a decade or two under their belt may be able to shed some light on your particular experience.

In general, whatever is happening, allow it to move through you and don't create any drama around it or create a story about it. Just let it be.

There are times though when strangeness on the mat needs to be addressed. Sometimes, we make groaning or guttural sounds when we're struggling, striving or trying too hard. Those sounds can be a signal that we need to back off, find our breath, and approach the postures with softness. A good teacher will be able to discern the difference between sounds (is it spontaneous releases or over-exertion?) and give you appropriate guidance. Over time, by tuning in and paying attention to the sounds you're making, you too will be able to tell the difference and adjust accordingly.

Different postures affect us all differently depending on what parts of the body are opening and releasing, or which energy centres are being activated. Here's a list of some of the more common experiences during postures you're likely to encounter in a yoga class. It's not an exhaustive list, but covers a few common experiences.

Deep Hip Openers like Pigeon Pose often bring us to tears – thankfully we're already bowing deeply to the ground so can privately let go into our emotions.

Backbends are one of the most common postures to trigger emotional releases. After all, they're opening our hearts right up! Sometimes too, we can feel dizzy or nauseous coming out of a back bend like Camel, Bridge or Wheel.

Sometimes it's the simple postures that can trigger a release – Child's Pose or Shavasana. We're often finally allowing ourselves to settle and soften into the moment and our emotions – which may have been released earlier in class – catch up with us.

Any practice that uses sound – chanting, mantras or loud breath like Lion's Breath – can also release emotion. Sometimes, it's an enjoyable emotion like joy and bliss. Sometimes it's all the anger we've never expressed throughout our lifetime. It depends largely on the person, the situation and the yoga.

As a beginning student, the most important thing is to understand that whatever experience you're having, it's okay. It means the yoga is working. Secondly, you want to make sure you're in a class situation where you feel supported and safe. Finally, sometimes yoga can dig up such intense emotions that it can be useful to work with a professional in a therapy session to deal with the accompanying memories or experiences. Yoga does stir up our psyche and the practice is not always enough as we work through some of the deeper aspects of our being. If you find your yoga practice is throwing you off kilter or psychologically taking you places you don't want to go alone – find yourself a good therapist and do the work of yoga and the work of therapy together. They're a great complement!

Forget about everybody else: find your centre

Walking into yoga class for the first time is a frightening experience. Not only is the room or studio likely to be unfamiliar, but so are the people, the teacher, the clothing, the props, the language, the movements and the etiquette. Hopefully by now, you've got a clearer idea of some of these aspects of the yoga world. However, any new situation, no matter how much you research beforehand, is always going to generate some nerves.

I still get nervous walking into a new studio, even though I've been practicing yoga for over a decade. It's a normal and natural way to feel.

How much you're freaking out will depend on the kind of personality you have and how far out of your comfort zone yoga is. Likely, if you've done a lot of dance, aerobics, martial arts and performance arts, you'll feel okay about going to yoga class.

However, if you've never been that physical or feel physically different to your perception of the average yogi – older, larger, tighter – you're more likely to experience some serious nerves.

You may feel like you stick out like a sore thumb – that everybody else is in the groove and it's really obvious you're brand new and don't know what to do.

And maybe that's true.

Maybe, if someone else was looking around the room and paying close attention, they would notice that you're new to yoga.

But even if they did, in general, most other yoga students are excited that someone is giving yoga a go for the first time. They're supportive, encouraging and kind. At least, that's been my experience in the classes I've been to in years gone past. In fact, there are still situations when I feel like a total newbie.

Recently I went to an Ashtanga Mysore style class with a teacher I didn't know, hosted by another teacher I didn't know, in a room I'd never done yoga in before with people I didn't know.

Mysore-style Ashtanga is self-practice – that is, there's a set sequence, the ashtanga sequence, and everybody goes through that sequence at their own pace. I walked into the room not really knowing the sequence, hoping I could just fake it by following the person next to me. Which I managed to do (kind of) – enough to get through the class.

There were a couple of factors that helped me make it through this class without collapsing into a bundle of nerves or freaking out that I was doing it wrong and everyone else knew and was secretly laughing at me.

They're the same key factors that you can use when you go to your first yoga classes. I say classes, because there's always more than one 'first yoga class'. There's the first class you ever go to, there's the first class you go to in a different location. There's the first class with a different teacher. There's the first class with a different style. All of those factors (location, teacher and style) slightly alter the situation you're walking into and therefore what's expected of you.

The most important factor to remember is this:

It's okay to be brand new and know absolutely nothing

By extension, it's okay to be you, just as you are. You'll feel uncomfortable and nervous, but that's okay.

Often, we have these outlandish expectations of ourselves and we don't even know it. Like we should be able to do every yoga posture in the class even though we've never done yoga before. Or that we should know what props we're meant to grab before class even though we've never done this class before. Or that we should know what those weird sounding words mean even though we've never heard them before.

How do you know if you're holding one or more of those unconscious expectations? When you're in your first class and can't get into one of the postures and you feel ashamed or guilty or bad about it. In those moments, you remind yourself of key factor #1 – it's okay to be a newbie. It's okay to not get into all the postures.

Or halfway through the class and the teacher says, "Now grab your strap from beside your mat." You realise that you have no strap beside your mat and you blush bright red and duck your head because you don't want people to see you're obviously new because you Didn't Get A Strap.

Again – this is when you take a deep breath and remind yourself. It's okay to not know everything. It's okay to forget props. It's okay – and so are you.

Or the teacher reels off an impossibly long-sounding name in Sanskrit and you have no idea what she's said or what it means and frantically look around the room at everyone else moving effortlessly into the next pose and you feel like you're in a secret club and no one's given you the password. It's okay.

Hell, often the teacher doesn't even know what the Sanskrit word actually means – he's just learned the sounds by rote and knows what posture it's referred to. He may even be flourishing the word like that because he thinks it makes him sound cool and knowledgeable. Take a deep breath, follow along with the other students, or if you're feeling really bold, attempt to get the teacher's attention and ask him to explain in English. Theoretically he should know you're new, he should be keeping an eye on you and theoretically, a great teacher will know what you want if you just stare intensely enough at him.

So that's Key Factor #1: It's okay to know nothing and you're okay just as you are. Use that as a mantra through your first classes, every time you feel awkward, ashamed, embarrassed or lost. Repeat to yourself, it's okay. I'm okay. Remember to breathe, right down into your belly. That will help shift your internal experience from fight or flight into relaxation.

Key factor #2 is that nobody is really looking at you and nobody really cares

Hard to believe, but true. Most people in a yoga class are completely focused on their own experience – that's what they're there for and that's what they're being trained to do – to stay in the moment, connected to their breath, with their attention completely on their internal experience. So even though you walk into class and you could swear that there's a huge red neon sign flashing above your head that screams 'I'm new and I don't know anything,' in reality, everyone's totally self-absorbed in their own experience. So when you feel nervous or concerned or anxious; remind yourself that nobody is looking and nobody cares.

However, there are exceptions to this rule. Some people will notice and some people do care. These people fall into two camps. The supportive, helpful folk who will lean over and whisper "We usually use straps and blocks in this class, you can grab them over there." And the rude, judgmental kind who look you up and down and sniff because you're wearing the wrong outfit, took their favourite mat spot or are deflecting the attention of the teacher they usually get.

The supportive, helpful folk are there to hold your hand and hopefully make you feel less nervous. They remember what it was like to be new. The rude, judgmental kind actually feel just as freaked out as you are, but their particular ego defence system comes in a different flavour – a rude and judgmental kind.

Regardless, the important thing to remember about the people who notice you're new? Their reaction is all about them and nothing to do with you. The kind and supportive people will be that way with everyone because that's how they like to be – they're empathetic or it makes them feel good to step into the role of Kind & Helpful. The rude and judgmental kind are that way with everyone because they're covering up their own nervousness, anxiety and issues of self-worth. *You* haven't done anything wrong. So if people do notice you and have some kind of reaction to you in the class – whether kind and helpful or rude and judgmental, repeat this mantra to yourself. 'It's all about them. It's all about them. I'm okay. I'm okay.'

Those are two key factors that will help you get through your first class. You thought there might be more? No, it's pretty damn simple. You're okay, and any reaction from another person is all about them. Unless of course you step on their foot as you walk past because you're so worried about where to put your mat. Then it's also about you. An apology would be necessary!

The most important thing is to keep coming back to your experience and your breath. In fact, you could say that your yoga began the moment you walked in the door – not when the teacher started teaching. Just as in yoga postures, as you walk in and get settled, pay attention to your breath, notice the thoughts and feelings that arise but just let them go, and keep coming back to your breath. If needed, repeat this in your mind, just like it's a mantra:

'I'm okay.'

'It's okay to be new.'

'I'm okay.'

Because you are, and it is.

CONCLUSION: FINDING TIME, MAKING TIME, HANGING IN THERE

Before you start yoga or when you've only been to a few classes, it seems like this entire new world that you stand outside of, like a small child, nose pressed against the window, watching these other students laughing and relaxed, moving effortlessly from one posture to the next... how could you possibly ever feel comfortable there?

But you will, in time, class by class, practice by practice. Until one day you turn around and realise you couldn't conceive of a life without yoga. You realise you feel comfortable and at ease in most classes, if not yet in the postures. You realise that you can do this – you can learn yoga. The strange words and movements and ideas no longer seem quite as strange.

Yet despite this – despite what yoga does for your body, mind and soul – it's likely that you may stop going for a week, a month, a year or even a decade.

Life happens. We get busy. We move. Our budget shifts. Stepping back into class and back into practice can sometimes be harder than when we first went to yoga. We feel guilty – like we've let down yoga and let down the yoga world. We worry about everything we might have forgotten or how our bodies might have seized up in the meantime. These worries and fears can make it hard to get back to class.

But get back to class you must, because that is yoga. It's showing up, again and again and again no matter how uncomfortable it is or how awful it is. It's staying with the process, no matter what comes up.

Yoga is a journey from the self to the Self, and the terrain you journey over is that of the psyche. All those buried emotions, memories and thoughts have to be felt, faced and released. All those defence mechanisms you mistake for who you are have to be seen and released. This is difficult work and it takes great courage.

Sometimes, just when our practice is going really well, we turn around and realise we haven't been to yoga in a month. Why is that we wonder? Often, it's because we were about to break through into new territory and subconsciously, that's scary.

Subconsciously, the ego or small self doesn't want to break through into new territory – it wants to stay right here, in sight of the shore where it's safe thank you very much. But if we are to discover the true depths of who we are, we must leave the shore and strike out into the unknown. We must face the uncertainty.

It's the times when you stop going that are the most precious – that's when you need to get back to yoga as soon as possible. As soon as you notice, as soon as you're aware, as soon as you can. Don't worry about how long it's been – just show up again and keep showing up. Find time in your day and in your week, however you can. There's always a way.

In time, you'll start a home yoga practice because you can't always get to class, and because you want to spend time connecting to that deeper part of you. There's magic in a home practice because you are thrown back completely on your own resources. Oh, the voice of the teacher might be in your head, guiding you through the postures you learned in class, but it's you and only you showing up to your mat every morning.

Even with a solid home practice though, going to class and working with a teacher is still valuable. A good teacher will hold a mirror up to you and show you the bits of you that you don't see. Where you're holding, where you're forgetting to hold, where you need to let go, where you need to surrender. A teacher helps to keep you accountable too, especially through those tough times when old emotions come up, or long forgotten memories arise. Or when you realise that the idea you had in your head of who you are isn't true. That's when a good teacher can help to keep you steady.

Not everyone will walk this path – not everyone wants to know or face themselves. It can be so much easier to turn away and just keep living life as it always was. But sometimes, life doesn't let us do that either. Yoga keeps showing up. There are people I know who tell me they've been meaning to try yoga for five years, or ten years.

'I really must give yoga a go...'

Yet they don't. Even though they know it would be great for them, even though they're interested, even though they want to... they don't go. Why is that? It's because a part of them knows deep down that going to yoga is not always easy and they're afraid of what they might find when they get there. They're afraid of looking like a fool in a room full of lithe, bendy strangers. They're afraid of wearing the wrong clothing or being too fat or too old or too inflexible.

Some of those people will never make it to yoga. You might even be one of those people. You might have been meaning to go to yoga for a long time.... And now, here you are reading a book about going to yoga. It's the first step. Now you just need to show up to class and keep showing up to class.

Take a deep breath, right down into the pit of your belly. Let your belly expand and your pelvis release into your chair. Allow your ribs to expand but keep your shoulders soft and down. Feel that breath inside of you, expanding you outward. Exhale slowly, engaging the belly against the spine as you do so, until all of the air has left... and pause... before allowing the inhale to naturally arise and fill up the top of the lungs, middle of the lungs, bottom of the

lungs.... Belly expanding, pelvis releasing, ribs opening... Exhale....
All the way... belly meets spine.... Ah....

There.

That's yoga.

Being with your breath. Being with your body. Being with You.

Why wouldn't you want to be with You? Why wouldn't you
want to Be?

Know too that yoga takes time – it's not a one-time deal, a one-
month deal or even a one-decade deal. It's a lifetime of showing up
to the mat, to class and to yourself.

I took my first class in 1995 – a ten week course. I knew in that
moment that yoga was going to be profoundly important in my
life. Yet I didn't make it back to my next class until about 2000.
A four year gap! Then I did two classes, walked out of the second, and took another year gap. I signed up for a ten week course.
Stopped for another few months. Started sporadically going to
Bikram classes. It wasn't until 2004 that I established any kind of
consistent practice – that's eight years after my first yoga class.

So go easy on yourself. Don't expect to dive straight into yoga
and master it within the first month, year or decade. You'll start
and you'll stop. Now, it's rare that I miss a day. Yoga has become
the very ground of my life-force. Wherever I am, there is yoga. It's
in the way I write, the way I parent, the way I listen, the way I shop,
the way I am.

One day it may just be the way that you are too.

May your yoga practice support you as you journey inwards to
that which you truly are.

ACKNOWLEDGEMENTS

This was the book that happened almost by accident, yet would not have come into being without support from many people.

The Yoga Lunchbox community initiated this project, as people kept asking me to write a book they could give to their friends who wanted to try yoga but were too intimidated to walk into a studio. It seemed like a great idea and when I did some research I couldn't find anything already fitting this description. So big thanks to all those people who leave comments, write emails, send me texts and talk to me in person – your feedback is invaluable.

The editing process was helped among by my devoted beta-readers, Sara Foley and Lu Cox. They were joined by two new beta-readers Kierin Smart and Clowance Nolan. All four provided excellent feedback that honed the book and it's scope.

Amanda Reid provided astute feedback on the accuracy (or otherwise!) of my dates, history and philosophy. I'm not a yoga scholar and she graciously talked me through some nuances of lineages and styles that I'd glossed over. Any remaining errors are all mine.

Book titles and subtitles are often difficult to determine and I struggled with this book. Fortunately Melissa Billington was able to help out by suggesting ten or so options for a subtitle – one of which won out.

Yvonne Kerr provided an expert editorial eye and pointed out that some of my esoteric language might lose those new to yoga – the exact opposite of my intention.

My book designer Kelly Spencer delivered an exceptional result and I did a whoop of joy when I saw her final book cover – she's made the content of the book come alive.

Matthew Bartlett held the entire process together, handling all the layout and final design elements, plus managing the print process for me. His expertise always makes me feel like I'm in the realms of the big publishing houses.

As always I've had out-standing support from my family and friends over the year it took to birth this book – there's been discussions on what it's like to be brand new to yoga, feedback on book cover roughs, plus general hand-holding and cheerleading.

Finally, I want to thank my son, Samuel. He's only four years old but constantly provides me with opportunities to practice my yoga in the best possible way and he's great at initiating plenty of fun and making sure life is not all about work.

This book would never have happened without the input from all of these people, and many more. This is collaborative, community-based publishing at its best.

ABOUT THE AUTHOR

Kara-Leah Grant is a yoga teacher and writer living in New Zealand. She's the editor of *The Yoga Lunchbox*, New Zealand's online yoga magazine and the mother to a young ninja warrior. Writing has always been a big passion – she self-published her first novel at age 12, a high suspense crime thriller driven by a strong female protagonist and antagonist. This is Kara-Leah's second book and she's already contemplated what to write for the third, although it's unlikely to be a crime thriller. You can contact her directly at: klgrant@fastmail.fm